Opposite Sex

Opposite

GAY MEN ON LESBIANS, LESBIANS ON GAY MEN

Sex

Edited by

Sara Miles and Eric Rofes

New York University Press

NEW YORK AND LONDON

NEW YORK UNIVERSITY PRESS
New York and London

Library of Congress Cataloging-in-Publication Data
Opposite sex : gay men on lesbians, lesbians on gay men / edited by Sara Miles and Eric Rofes.
p. cm.
Includes index.
ISBN 0-8147-7476-8 (clothbound : acid-free paper).—ISBN 0-8147-7477-6 (paperback : acid-free paper)
1. Homosexuality. 2. Gays—Sexual behavior. 3. Gay-lesbian relationships. I. Miles, Sara, 1952– . II. Rofes, Eric E., 1954– .
HQ76.25.066 1998
306.76′6—dc21 97-33960
CIP

New York University Press books are printed on acid-free paper, and their binding materials are chosen for strength and durability.

Manufactured in the United States of America

10 9 8 7 6 5 4 3 2 1

Contents

Introduction

Sara Miles and Eric Rofes

The past ten years have seen an extraordinary outpouring of research, writing, and talk about lesbian and gay sexuality,[1] triggered in part by the confluence of the AIDS epidemic, the feminist sex wars, and the development of queer studies. Academics and activists alike have delved into the contemporary and historical relationships between erotic desire and queer identities, cultures, and communities.

Yet as activists and writers ourselves and as participants in lesbian and gay study groups on sex and politics, we've been frustrated by recurring gaps and absences in the queer studies approach to sexuality, as well as by the limitations of queer community discourse on sex. We began work on this anthology hoping to address some of the elements missing from discussions of lesbian and gay sexuality. Two areas in particular became the central focus for *Opposite Sex*.

The first was sex itself: in queer studies, we saw flesh and fluids increasingly displaced by footnotes and the examination of lived sexual experience relegated to confessional narratives, popular journalism, or pornography. In *Opposite Sex,* we wanted to bring back the sex and make real bodies, acts, and desires central to analysis of lesbian and gay sexuality.

The other omission that our project confronted — an absence we'd noted in conversations and community dialogue as much as in academic work — concerns the relationships between male and female homosexualities. Despite the social reality of a gay and lesbian community, there has been a remarkable dearth of thoughtful discourse about the many ways lesbians and gay men are implicated in each other's (supposedly separate) sexual realities. What does it mean, we wanted to know, that some lesbians enjoy viewing gay male porn videos? Why do some gay men love to read through the lesbian personal ads? What kinds of identity shifts occur when lesbians and gay men have sex with each other? We found few lesbians writing or talking about gay male sex and sex cultures; gay men rarely even referenced lesbian sexuality in their explorations of the intersection of sex and culture.

As we solicited work, these issues kept resurfacing. It was striking how many queer writers could critically examine the most controversial aspects of lesbian and gay politics yet still be uncomfortable publishing any of their views about the other gender's sexuality. Some of the reluctance may have been based on the feeling that cross-gender dialogue about sex (especially homosexual sex) is heretical; some may have stemmed from aversion to explicit discussions of bodies and sexual practices. (Gay men, in particular, seemed to find it extremely difficult to talk directly about lesbian sex.) We had to insist repeatedly that we were not looking for reflections on lesbian and gay "community" (or, in the more romanticized version of the rhetoric, "family,") but for discussions of lesbian and gay sex.

The contributors to *Opposite Sex* ground their work in readings of real bodies, practices, and sex cultures. At the same time, they refuse to quarantine sex or to theorize sexuality apart from issues of power, politics, economics, and social organization. The chapters in this book examine the complex, visceral, and difficult questions that lesbians and gay men confront as they seek to understand each other, such as

- What do we see when we see each other? Are gay men sexually "men" to lesbians, lesbians "women" to gay men, or is there a uniquely queer, particularly "gay" or "lesbian" sexual expression that we see?
- Just as one element of a gay or lesbian sexual identity involves being not straight, does part of a lesbian sexual identity also revolve around being not a gay man? Are gay men defined as not lesbian? Or is an erotic identification with the homosexual of the opposite sex a key element in the construction of our (homo)sexualities?
- What is it about the other's desire that lets us know our own? What is learned, taught, copied, or ignored?
- How does the image of the other enter our own sexual imagination and practice? How does the actual other enter our own sexual lives?

Opposite Sex contains writing by lesbians and gay men about experiences with each other's bodies, interpretations of different male and female homosexual sex cultures, and reflections on the history, sociology, and politics of the changing discourses about queer sexuality. We believe *Opposite Sex* shows the rich and complex ways in which individuals and communities make meaning from their quotidian sexual impulses, their utopian sexual mores, and their idiosyncratic sexual acts.

This anthology draws on the work of scholars and academics, artists, historians, and journalists, as well as the lesbian and gay activists whose practices create the ground for theory. We have benefited in particular from the contributions of our lovers—Martha Baer, who named this book, and Crispin Hollings, who helped conceptualize it—and the members of our Sex/Pol study groups, who showed us what can happen when gay men and lesbians talk about sex together. We thank them all and hope their diverse voices will continue to expand our understanding of all the sexual selves, lives, and cultures we are creating.

Notes

1. With some uneasiness, we've decided to use the term *lesbian and gay* in the anthology's subtitle and in this introduction. This book is written by and about people who variously identify themselves as lesbian, gay, bisexual, transgendered, queer, and combinations thereof, as well as by people who reject those choices. We find all the available nomenclature problematic: "lesbian and gay" suggests exclusion; "queer" slides over differences; and lists like "lesbian/gay/bi/trans" tend to expand into increasingly detailed taxonomies of identity without helping explain the system of classification. Since we see no single

correct way to adequately describe the range of sexual identities represented in this book, we've decided to follow the basic principle of self-determination, which holds that a "bisexual," "lesbian," "transsexual," "gay," "homosexual," "queer," or, for that matter, a "heterosexual" is anyone who chooses that name.

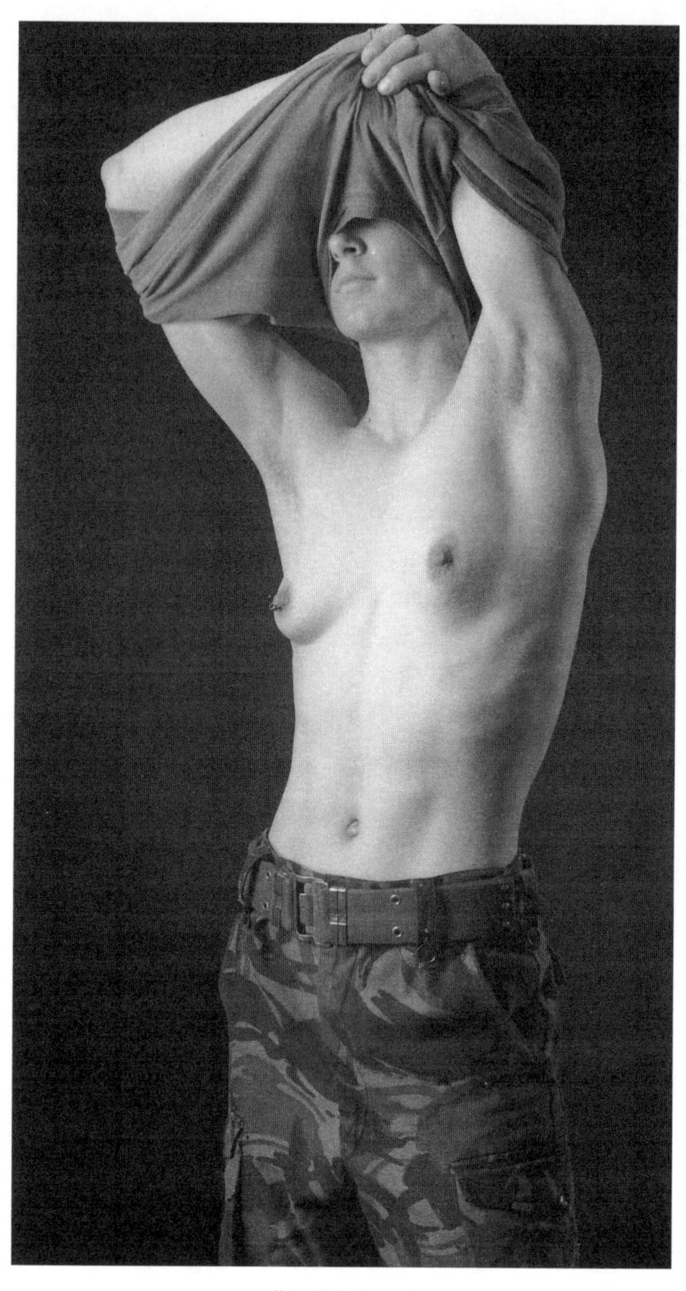

"Jackie" (1993)
Della Grace

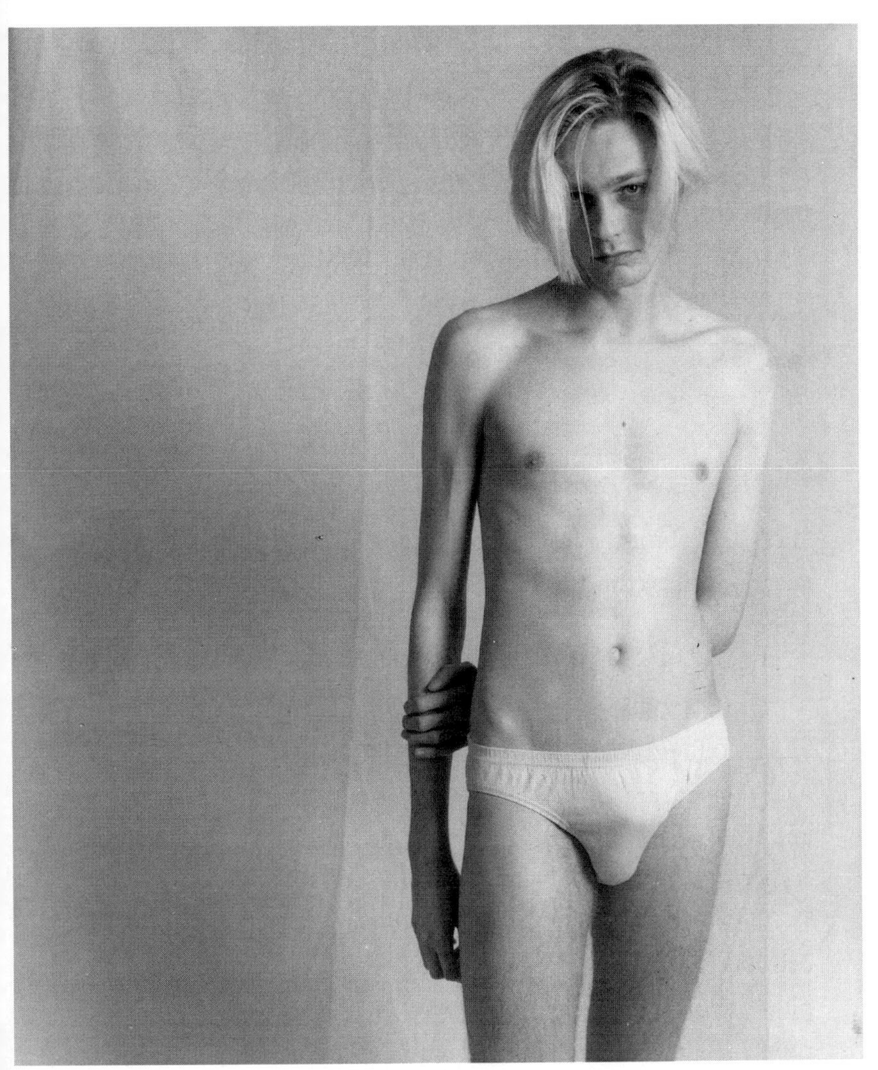

"Lee, the Boy" (1994)
Della Grace

C H A P T E R

Blackbeard Lost

Linnea Due

"Let's talk about fisting as an instance of cultural migration," I suggest to the crowd of older leather dykes gathered around the buffet table.

"Where's it migrating from?" asks Tina.

"Or to?" Sukie wants to know.

The others, aware of my tendency to be pedantic about unlikely topics, are superintending a more vital transfer of pasta and fruit salad to paper plates. "Tell the truth, girls," I challenge, suspecting I'm in for a fight. "When did you first hear the word?"

I heard about fisting first in sixties-era gay male S/M porn, a delirious world where naive young men get spirited away to pirate ships, deserted islands, wretched basements, and back rooms of bars to be tortured and repeatedly despoiled by a rogue's gallery of revolting but manly hunks with big big pricks and even bigger fists, which they sink up to the armpit in our quivering hero's sweetly puckered virgin ass (newly virginal every time, because each successive hunk is grosser and more gargantuan than the last mammoth monster). Our hero, who has no choice, nevertheless becomes redeemed through his ability to endure these enormous intrusions into his deepest, darkest center. In fact, very soon this quailing, sobbing boy realizes his trials are a matter of honor, of courage, of manliness itself: only a man can take what these brutes dish out. He's transformed from a boy pretending to be a man to a man strong enough to be a boy in the company of men.

But in the sixties, for me, all this was about as attainable as waking up in the middle of *The Story of O*. That didn't stop me from trying—since age seventeen I'd been storming gay male leather bars and being tossed out on my ear more times than I wanted to remember. Why was I so obsessed with Folsom Street? Perhaps because it was the only game in town for a budding leather queer, and my fantasy life, perhaps because of the pirates, was heavy on male bonding. But even my gay guy pals couldn't get into Fe-Be's: they were too nelly, too vanilla, too Night of the Living Clones. So when, at the close of the 1970s, via the ministrations of SAMOIS, I ventured into the heretofore male preserves of the Catacombs and the Cauldron, knowing these clubs were proving grounds for the FFA (not the Future Farmers of America), it was like reaching nirvana.

Admittedly, most of the play parties I went to at the Catacombs or the Cauldron were mixed or women's events, with men in not much more than token attendance. Still, I saw where the men partied, and I imagined what they did.

Picture a roomful of slings. A St. Andrew's cross or two. A cage. A bathtub. A horse. Several leather-covered tables with convenient handles and straps. All in black-painted rooms with booming sound systems and indirect lighting. The only time you wanted light glaring in your eyes was if you'd been captured by the Gestapo and it was part of the ambience.

Mostly there were slings upon slings upon slings—in the Catacombs an entire row of them. Clearly a lot of fucking was going on. Certainly there was with the girls. People arrived early and began setting up at one sling or another. Hanging up the crop there, setting the can of Crisco here. The fact that Crisco was thoroughly gross to put up your cunt didn't matter; it was what the guys used.

Everyone had been indoctrinated with proper fisting hygiene. You cut your nails, then you cut your nails again, and then you filed them. And after you finished filing, you dragged the tips of your fingers across your skin, and if you could sense that a nail ever existed, you went back to the file. When surgical gloves came in on the heels of safer sex, the irritation of wearing them was tempered by the thrill of once again being able to pick up a piece of paper.

It's hard to convey how pandemic all this activity at the slings was, how social (how many dykes does it take to fist-fuck one writhing, rapt woman?), how emblematic of the play parties of that era. In those early days, the fistees laid down an almost solid layer of background orgasming, a euphoric cacophony of sobs, shrieks, and howls, an aural flying carpet that snatched you up and carried you to heaven, where you could listen to women coming all night long, one after another, again and again and again.

But something confused me. Why were fisting and S/M birds

of a feather, always flocking together? Granted, pointing your heels at the ceiling and making like a wishbone would have to be chalked on the submissive side of the ledger, and the fistee's humiliating position lent itself to all sorts of fiendish entertainments. But these possibilities seemed to depend more on the sling than on the fist, and it was the latter that received the emphasis, in both word and deed.

The link made more sense to me when it came to the guys. I only had to remember the pirates parading in with their hamlike hands and short, thick forearms, our boy's hopeless pleas for mercy, his eyes rolling in terror, and those stumpy arms pumping furiously. . . .

Did my confusion hang on the assumption that boys aren't supposed to be fucked and girls are? Was it about the ecstasy of cunts and the agony of assholes? Certainly there are plenty of dykes who don't like vaginal penetration and live for being ass-fucked. Not to put too fine a point on it, I only had to look to my own predilections to debunk the agony/ecstasy theory. Maybe it was just that those girls in the slings didn't look frightened or discomfited in the least. Enthralled was more like it.

Did the guys look terrified? Did they have the grace and goodwill to pretend to be terrified? Or were they greedy little slut pigs like the girls? I lost my innocence when I admitted there are no pirates and no quaking boys, only aspirants to the throne of the salacious and the ravenous.

Soon enough, fisting started to migrate and, in the process, cast off its unseemly roots. First it was only those rotten claiming-to-be-feminist leather dykes who would do something so male (and gay male, at that). Then fisting began being written about in dyke mags like *Bad Attitude* and *On Our Backs*. The latter had "how to" articles; the former took it for granted. Various sexperts took fisting on the road, and it was one of the most asked questions on nearly anyone's book tour, even if your book was about growing dyke asparagus. For a while, fisting was racy and rad in Lesbianland, sort of like French kissing when you were twelve, except you're thirty-five. Now, of course, fisting has un-transgressed to the status of summer reruns: ho-hum. It's been reduced to thrilling the likes of homophobe Peter LaBarbera, who reprints those how-to pieces in his rag *Lambda Report*, which purports to tell the Moral Majority what those filthy gays have up their sleeves.

This, then, is the road map I lay out to my bemused pals around the buffet. "See how the same act can take on and lose significance depending on who's performing it?" I ask. "It moves from taboo to mundane, from chocolate to vanilla. In fact, *migration* is the wrong word. *Colonization* might be better since it's never left where it's been, it just assumes a different guise."

"Exactly!" Lee says. "And where it's been is among dykes for umpteen generations." On this we're all willing to agree: dykes (and unlabeled and labeled others) have incorporated fist fucking into lovemaking since the dawn of hands and cunts and assholes.

"But sliding your hand up someone's cunt until it curls into a fist is different from making fisting a separate, ritualized act," Tina argues.

"Is it?" Lisa asks. "Why?"

Two women admit they never heard of fisting in either context until they encountered it in the hallowed halls of the Catacombs. Lee is shaking her head. "What we're saying is to name it is to claim it," she points out. "If we call something *we* do the word they call it, then it seems as if *they* invented it."

"Once something is named, it changes forever," Lisa says. "It can become a fetish; it can become an event. It takes on a life of its own."

The next morning, a Sunday, the phone rings at seven. My girlfriend answers. "It's Sukie," she shouts into the bedroom. "She says that Lee remembered when she first heard the word *fisting*."

"Good," I mutter.

"Sukie says Lee was so upset she stayed up half the night trying to remember, and finally she did. The first time she heard anyone use the word was in a conversation at a lesbian communal house in Berkeley in the spring of 1971. She's certain it wasn't used in connection with either gay men or S/M, and they were talking about the specific act."

"Mmm."

"She remembers it was that spring because she moved to Oregon that summer, and she distinctly recalls that she heard the word before she moved to Oregon."

"Uh-huh." The pillow is over my head.

"Lee wanted to make sure you knew that fisting has *nothing* to do with gay men and never did."

"Check."

Clear as Crisco. But I don't mind. What I wish is that we could have back those endless nights at the Catacombs along with the innocence and spirit and vision underneath. I wish that dykes and fags could have come together, as we were beginning to, around life and sex instead of around death. I wish those guys could tell me when *they* first heard the word.

And I wish there were pirates.

CHAPTER 

GM ISO (m)other: A Gay Boy in the World of Lesbian Personals

Francisco J. Gonzalez

Skip past the news in almost any gay rag to the backroom of the paper: the personal ads. After you've read the downcast reports from the front—the scuttlebutt and scandal, the latest dirt on HIV policy or same-sex marriage—the polysemous voice of the community speaks for itself, looking for connections, for a scene. The personal ad lets you feel that you're fishing in open waters, unconstrained by quotidian social networks. That Other of your dreams, the one you might never bump into at the club, might just be the queer next door, who, tantalized by your pithy and seductive self-encapsulation, nibbles, takes the hook, and voilà! fantasy unlimited.

Beyond the pragmatics of cruising, the writing and reading of want ads also defines a space in gay community. Virtuality without electronics, personals are an imaginary field of possibility sustained by allure—with luck, the word might just become flesh. In contrast to other fantasy venues like old-fashioned prostitution and much of the phone-sex industry in which money buys sexual goods, the personal ads keep costs down by giving the buyer only the right to barter. Compared with the technological support required for Internet surfing, the MasterCard numbers needed for phone fantasies, or the wad of cash for a hot escort, admission to the world of the want ads is trifling.

The personals constitute a marketplace that resides in a collective imaginary. Its geography is amoebic, limited and sustained by the materiality of the newspaper's circulation. Every now and then, an ad makes the discontinuities clear in the fine print: Must be willing to relocate.

Beyond the traffic of actual bodies, the personals are a New Market of the networking city, a symbolic economy of the mind, to borrow from Samuel Delany, in which sales are based not on "knowledge of goods" but on "questions of taste."[1] In this virtual market, the conventional privacy of sexual solicitation goes queerly public. Public in a particular way, however, because the personal ad both reveals and conceals the seller, and the reader remains a potential buyer who doesn't materialize until a counteroffer is made. In this virtual cruising ground, a gay man can go browsing in lesbian desire: a nosy neighbor with his ear to the wall.

I had been reading gay men's ads for years, but reading lesbian personals provided a new thrill. As a disembodied reader, I was the perfect voyeur, all eyes, intercepting love letters meant for another. But a look, as we all know this late in the twentieth century, is neither simple nor innocent. Stealing glimpses of another changes your relationship to yourself. As a gay man looking in on lesbian cruising, I began imagining lesbian scenes inscribed in my own (homo)sexuality.

When I read the personals, when the pure pleasure is in the reading, I want the ad to arrest me. I want to be recognized. I cruise the field, the smudge of ink on my fingers dulling the newsprint, looking for myself, for a reification of my fantasy scene. An ad sparks my attention because it provides a translation (confirmation) of my imaginary in the community symbolic. A glancing detail can illuminate desire. I still remember a *Honcho* ad in the late 1970s: a short, "humpy," guy looking for a lover—"I get enuf tricks at the bar." Was it idealized identification with the "short and humpy" that got me? Or the "enuf" (blue-collar butch and schoolgirlish all at once) that seemed to promise excess? I had a lover and the relationship was sinking fast. The ad allowed me a view of the other side: I could fill the shoes of a hot little number careening from one liberating sexual encounter to another, all longing. I had no interest in calling him up or becoming his lover; the moment of pleasure was recognition, of him as a character in one of the movie scripts of my desire.

In their seminal essay "Fantasy and the Origins of Sexuality," Laplanche and Pontalis argue that fantasy is the structural foundation of subjectivity. Following Freud (in *Instincts and Their Vicissitudes*), they view sexuality as an effect of psychic representation. Fantasy, the unfolding sexual mental text, is the scene or setting of desire. In this foundational narrative, the subject is not in the position of a particular player or role or even in the movements and action flowing between players:

> Fantasy, however, is not the object of desire, but its setting. In fantasy the subject does not pursue the object or its sign: he appears caught up himself in the sequence of images. He forms no representation of the desired object, but is himself represented as participating in the scene. . . . As a result, the subject, although always present in the fantasy, may be so in a desubjectivized form, that is to say, in the very syntax of the sequence in question.[2]

I read the sex ad as an attempt to capture such a phantasmatic sequence in text, to present an alluring "de-subjectivized" subject. As want ad convention has it, the writer of the ad sends out a message to the great maw of Otherness, waiting for the processed, articulated confirmation of desire. The writer here is in the guise of the one in search of, the one who puts out the call, the subject looking for a sexual object. But isn't it really the writer who is called? Hasn't the disembodied voice of the Other already required: Who are you? What do you want? To which the writer of the ad dutifully responded by packing herself or himself densely into cryptogrammatics—SBiF, TV, bl/bl, Gr/p; the list multiplies daily[3]—a neat representation that can efficiently be put into circulation. Readers responding to a particular ad find some point of homology or identification with the scene presented; the fantasy activates their own imaginary script. It's frisson: desubjectivized subjects rubbing up against each other. As sexual scenes, personal ads encapsulate—albeit watered-down, mediated, transformed, or hyperbolized—foundational fantasies.

Such fantasies are not essentially hardwired, prebuilt into the subject, or biological, as Laplanche and Pontalis note: originary fantasies are "actualized and transmitted by the parental fantasies." In the early physical relationship with another body, the nascent subject begins to read the inscriptions of an external touch that actualizes sexuality. The "intrusion" of the mother (in the form of her body, fantasy, and desire) into the infant world sets off the dynamo of sexual longing. I will have more to say later about this hazy origin. But parental fantasies also operate in a less physical way to "transmit" available social registers of fantasy scripts and scenarios. They are fantasies in history as well as historically constitutive of the subject. Fantasy, in other words, is activated from outside the subject and is not just an individual production but a social one as well.

Personal ads straddle these intrapsychic and social arenas, written in private but consumed in public, mass-produced but inexpensive and accessible, transient but leaving an inky trace that lasts at least until the recycling bin. Personals constitute a middle ground in the social construction of queer sexuality, not big-budget cultural representation (like film or the Internet, for example, or even books) but nonetheless a privileged place in gay community where fantasies are screened for public consumption. They consolidate and disseminate a lexicon of available fantasy categories in the chatty voice of the many, unfiltered by an interpretive discourse. Reading lesbian ads (re)activated my fantasies: the social formulas of the personals gave way to the idiosyncrasies of desire.

Lesbian Circuitry

Lesbian sex ads were at first not easy to come by. The back pages of most gay newspapers offered copious black-and-white photos of burly smiling massage therapists and personals soliciting everything from girlie boys in panties to a wide assortment of foot admirers. There were few women seeking women.

Gay male ads are notoriously full of fetish detail. In this market, the penis is the commodity of choice. Of course you can find ads for long walks on the beach and fireplace romance, but sexual acts are frequently spelled out, specified. The presence of daddy looms large: masochistic bottoms abound, looking to serve big-dicked tops with flattops; oily bodybuilders search for worshipers. A typical ad opens with body stats, describes the scene, and specifies the physical requisites of the other:

> *Big Man Seeks Daddy's Boy*
>
> Me: bld/blu, short beard, balding, 39, 5'11", 285#, bulk-mail looks, hairy, gdlkng, 7 1/2 uncut. You: smaller, hairy, hungry, & horny. Wants to take daddy's dick all the time. No drugs, fems, hustlers. Hairy butt big +.

The body is extensively cataloged; almost every ad in the sex section of the personals makes at least passing mention of chests, butts, dicks, arms, legs, feet, or hands. There is no shortage of descriptors: how bulky or slim or muscled or skinny the body is, the size of its parts, its hairiness or smoothness, whether it is tattooed or pierced, how the hair is cut (flattop, long, short, balding, shaved), how veiny or thin or big the arms are, whether the belly is washboard or beer gutted, whether the face is clean shaven, mustached, goateed, or bearded. Sexual positions and roles have been extensively codified. Fellatio (aka French active and passive and usually designated FrA, FrP) and anal penetration (aka Greek active and passive, or GrA, GrP) form the cornerstone of the code. Men's ads are virtual cryptograms of desire.

Such is not the case for women's ads. When I started reading lesbian personals, I couldn't help it; I kept looking for the missing phallus. Or for some shred of fetish. I stumbled across ads wanting "affectionate, loving, honest, passionate, monogamous relationships"—where was the meat? But something in the women's personals nagged me. They tended less toward the formulaic, more toward the elusive. Less sexual, more sexy. They stirred my envy of women who can get away with wearing slinky black cocktail dresses. They offered something that continually just exceeded my grasp, and as desire would dictate, this turned me on. But perversely perhaps, I couldn't quite put my finger on it. I felt the space between me and the fantasy, between me and the text, between me and the female body:

Hardcover Seeks Softcover

Voracious reader/redhead devours books nightly, but no matter how firmly I hold one between my hands or how deeply I bury my face in the page, I never come up wet—only well read. Help me flesh out some of my favorite titles: the passion, sexing the cherry, written on the body. Magic password that makes this big, brazenly butch top weak kneed: nice Jewish girl who isn't.

When I tried to intercalate myself in the devouring fantasy of the redhead, I felt I was poking, hopelessly male. I was—obviously, stupidly—locked out of what seemed a logic of specular desire: women seeking women.

I went to the Castro branch of the public library. Whisking through a year (1993 was available in full that day) of *Deneuve* personals left me with little more than the standard formula: X seeks Y and an extensive tabulation of pedestrian likes and dislikes. "Music" (folk, alternative, country, classical, light rock) was the most popular avocation, followed closely by "reading/books/literature" and "arts/sculpture/photography." There was the expected passion for long walks in the park, "allover tans," and "mornings, laughter, and imagination." Melissa Ethridge, Martina, k. d., and the Indigo Girls loomed on the horizon of unattainable desirables. Occasionally there was a line that promised the erotic story. The Central NY BI who wanted to "teach young femme just as [she] was taught by equally sensitive mentor," or the Boston Femme "looking for leather lez who loves . . . lacy lingerie;" or the androgynously femmy butch who exhorted "no romance please." But largely the Deneuvian marketplace had more to offer in the way of "vegetarianism," "learning about people," and "new experiences" than it did about erotic encounters.

This is, no doubt, partially a function of class. Following Laura Kipnis's reading of *Hustler,* I read the desexualization of the *Deneuve* personals as a move away from blue collar and toward bourgeoisie.[4] In the trajectory of that analysis, *Hustler*'s sexual explicitness is masculinized pig lust and partial objects and codes blue-collar rejection of highbrow effetism, snobbery, and intellectualism. *Deneuve* is clearly not pornography, but its pristine personals seemed to me a complement to *Hustler*'s vulgarity: a solid claim to middle-class respectability. Economics certainly influence the narrower range of venues available to lesbians seeking sex. It's no surprise, for example, that lesbians are more likely to be dancing in an adult theater for straight men than for other lesbians: some men will pay the money, and some lesbians need the income.

The lesbian market may support fewer seamy sex venues, but they do exist. But these were not the pages of *Lezzie Smut* or *Venus Infers.* In the slick and mainstream-tending pages of *Deneuve,* rolling around in carnal knowledge would appear, well, crass.

The personals of local gay papers (from San Francisco, New York, Los Angeles) advertised more offers of out-and-out sex. More stirred by these ads, I found myself looking for vestigial remnants or promising clues of a phallic presence. At its most blatant, the phallus appeared in portable form and addressed me directly in one of the "bi" sections of the personals:

> *Have Strap-ons, Will Travel*
>
> Two, dominant dykes seek a submissive gay boy who's generous to a fault. Our dream gay boy will take us out to dinner often and spend money on us and then let us fuck him in the ass and mouth simultaneously. No hairy assholes. Must be clean shaven.

This was a place to start. In a boy-toy fantasy with a pecuniary twist, the "submissive gay boy" would play sugar daddy stripped of secondary sexual characteristics. At the restaurant, the trio would enact the trite ritual of masculine largesse (male economic power disguised as generosity "to a fault"?); at home, the gay boy would be a smooth, penetrable space.

The erotics of penetration brought the fantasy closer to home—it gave me an in. I began to recognize the lesbian phallus. In an ad entitled "Southwestern Fun" that after a typical list of

Californioid "likes" (horses, Buddhist meditation) provided the titillation: "Fantasize playing the saxophone. Size ten sneakers." Or in another ad: "Wanted: a Good Woman able to cook, clean, sew, dig worms, and have boat and motor. Please send picture of boat and motor to Daisy."

What appealed to me in these ads was the fetishistic shimmering of the phallus: now you see it, now you don't. It was there, making a displaced appearance in the saxophone, the size-queen sneakers, the boat and motor. More important, the boat and motor were simply the substitutions—with a voyeuristic photographic spin—of the Good Woman, herself the true phallus, the signifier of Daisy's desire. This figure of the good wife surfaced occasionally as a type of phallic being, the spectacular object of the desiring subject's gaze:

Hard Being Pretty

I want to cook, clean and be your wife. I'm the kind of girl you'll stare at all night but you are afraid to come up to me. I want to be loved, cared for, and kept. ISO attractive, feminine, or very soft butch GWF.

But if the lesbian phallus is present in these ads, it is a different kind of animal than the much ballyhooed penis. Male personal ads often stake out defining polarities along the binaries of top/bottom, active/passive, and master/slave; the relationship to the penis as phallus determines these positions. The top has it, the slave craves it. Lesbian ads de-center the male member. The boy-toy ad just mentioned, for example, divests the penis of its phallic significance. It's kinky gender: penetrating dykes transform the boy's manhood into a superfluous fleshy appendage. The penis in this scene is detachable and, as such, unnatural, reproducible, delightfully perverse.

The "good wife" ads queer gender more subtly, perhaps, but more profoundly. Whereas "wife" evokes the essential heterosexual paradigm—the "cooking and cleaning" object of her man's dominion—in these ads, the term equivocates, simultaneously eclipsing male presence. Daisy's good woman, a boat owner, butches it up digging worms but simultaneously cooks, cleans, and sews, a paradigm of stereotypical housewifely virtue. "Hard Being Pretty," an intimidating beauty with a phallic sheen, wants to be a wife and seeks a feminine husband to love her, care for, and keep her. In these ads, the category of "wife" is exploded in the refusal to accept an easy coequivalence of "wife" with "woman" and in the barring and erasure of male husbandry. In short, these ads contest and multiply conventional gender.

In the women's personals, in fact, gender position is the sine qua non. The scale runs from hard butch to pretty femme, fulcrumed on centrist androgyny. A "mid-20s SF andro-butch" seeking a "fun, warm-hearted dyke," writes that she is "most comfortable in flannel, T-shirts, and jeans" in a gender performance as fashion statement. Reworking a heteronormative view of "the opposite sex," the vectors of attraction in dyke gender run every which way. Femme, andro, and butch can come together in any combination of desiring subject and desired object. A "SGWF, upper 30s, 5'6", brown hair, blue-eyed, femme beauty," for example, seeks same:

You be SGWF, 30s, also very femme, beautiful, longer hair, sensually adventurous, enjoy cosmetic ware, be secure in what you want, and not afraid to peel back the fears. And you must be a good kisser! Are you ready?

Perhaps because femininity carries the mark of gender as the "other" in a male-dominated symbolic, lesbian personals are saturated by playful articulations of gender that simultaneously affirm and disavow the binarism of masculine/feminine. Here gender can eschew the logic of either/or; masculine and feminine are not compulsory opposites. Men's ads are more preoccupied with sexual aims and activities than with gender positions: the big question in men's ads is, Where does it go? In the women's ads, What is she wearing?[5] Gender is not a contested and therefore rich site of sexual production in men's ads. The drag queen and the girlie boy make rare appearances. When gender does surface, it's often to reinforce the masculine imperative, as in the anxious and almost ubiquitous exclusionary rule of men's ads in the late 1970s: No fats or fems. Gay male ads operate under the hegemonic sway of male power, and the result is a marketplace that values "straight-acting, straight-appearing" masculinity. Butch tops and butch bottoms.

The language of tops and bottoms originated in the S/M community but has been appropriated by many who wouldn't touch leather. When it intersects the lesbian gender spectrum, the code of dominance and submission makes for a dazzling array of sexual positions: slightly feminine tops, andro bottoms, dyke "daddies." And even though these combinations are certainly not the exclusive purview of the lesbian market (think of the prototypical straight dominatrix), their appearance in the personals demonstrates the extent of their codification as sexual positions, their density as loci in the lesbian symbolic.

One particularly striking position in this symbolic is the pivotal, and quintessentially lesbian, "switch," a role that toggles the femme/butch and top/bottom polarities. The switch, almost defined by her potential for movement, may operate more as a (de)stabilizing third term than as a center point in the spectrum. Like the category of "androgynous," "switch" questions the logic of a binarism by laying claim to both/neither of the polarities: the andro is both/neither butch/femme, the switch both/neither top/bottom:

True Switch

It's not that I'm into roles: I love them all! I'm just as happy butched out in my motorcycle leathers as I am femmed up in heels for a night on the town. Looking for a woman who can enjoy it all. . . . Don't really care what you do, as long as it's not excessive. Be: tall (5'6" minimum), strong (extra points if you can beat me at wrestling), playful, andro to butch, open to light S/M, and a top who can handle being flipped once in a while (cuz you know it's gonna happen. . .).

The injunction of the ending parentheses is coy recognition: you know, it seems to say, that these positions are fluid. In the logic of both/neither, the figure of the switch simultaneously affirms similarity and difference. In *The Practice of Love: Lesbian Sexuality and Perverse Desire,* Teresa de Lauretis describes the lesbian subject as caught up in a doubling and splitting, a reversible pattern of specularization and differentiation that presupposes at least two terms of the fantasy, two female bodies that are not simply the same but at once similar and different.[6]

The switch, as a structural position in lesbian sexuality, is anchored in this double movement of specularization and differentiation in which oscillation becomes play. The seeing and being seen of specularization, the mirroring identification with a similar body, promote fluidity. The switch can imagine herself in the other's body; she can see herself in the place of the one who simultaneously reflects her:

> *Would You Could You with a Witch*
>
> Would you could you be a switch? I do so like the taste of girl. I do so like a head of curls. Playful priestess-to-be wise in the ways of the world eager to meet mischievous femme who would warp her world view and ruffle her composure. Fluent in astrobabble. Flagrantly philosophical. Fiery for redheads. Awaiting adventure. All femmes need apply.

This ad is seduction theory with a kick: In the end the curly-headed femme, a wolf in girl's clothing, will flip the witch, leaving her authority warped and her composure ruffled. Here the switch is an object of desire by one worldly wise and philosophical who craves a little destabilization. In an ad that crosses Dr. Seuss with Hansel and Gretel, the evocation of childhood turns into a sexy bedtime story. Is it a stretch to read in the vacillations of the switch the dynamics of the mother–child bond?

Remembering Orality

Rewriting the past, imposing retroactive meaning, and suspecting origins may be elemental features of queerness. Coming out, for example, is simply a metaphor for the more significant process of capturing and naming (for better or for worse) the evolution of difference within normative sexuality. (Or social categories organize individual experience.) As such, coming out is subversive not because it actualizes gay identity politics but because it fundamentally challenges origins. It reads personal history retroactively, resetting the origins, upsetting teleology. In her essay "Suspended Beginnings: of Childhood and Nostalgia," Elspeth Probyn argues against a deterministic ordering of childhood experience, one that simply reconstructs and fixes the present.[7] Instead, she encourages us to queer childhood remembrance, to "start thinking about ways of using and recounting childhood outside of a regime of origins . . . to deny childhood its founding status . . . to rewind our stories, but not to recount them as links in a chronological chain that links the present to a fixed past" (p. 458). Remembering, Probyn might argue, is a construction, a fiction that weaves unsteadily between present and past, between a present irremediably stipulated by its past and a past always haunted by its construction in the present.

Reading lesbian personals got me thinking about childhood.

The switch ads, in particular, evoked mother–child narratives and the inevitable Oedipus. I thought of the "playful priestess-to-be" as some sort of Mommy-in-the-making wanting to seduce and be seduced by the little girl who would ineluctably "flip" her. The "wife" ads belied a parental presence, the ghost of mother—the original "good woman"—a hidden third term that fueled the syllogism of desire and made it cook. In some ads, the evocation of mother was more explicit: "This beautiful Mexican hot mama with lots of passion, healing hands and mouth, desires you." Sexual hunger—voracious and renewable—made frequent appearances in the personals, and oral sexuality emerged in some ads in a dizzying conflation of maternal imagery and nasty sex:

Horny Passion Flower

Looking for a fine woman of taste for Navajo Kitty. Are you hungry? Come and get it now. Right here right now.

If the penis-as-phallus was the flash point of the men's ads, then the mouth seems the heart of the matter for the lesbian personals. From the redhead devouring imagined lovers like books to the witch with a yen for a "taste of girl," I saw oral imagery flowering in the lesbian ads: a "soft attractive butch" seeks a "juicy, expressive femme" for "sweet affection," or "two bi busty girls who love to orally please one another" invite the curious to witness.

The mouth, one could say, remembers the mother. The surround of an imagined, longed-for, and irretrievably lost early sexual object, the mouth circumscribes absence. In the enjoyment that outstrips need (for food, for milk), doesn't orality capture an important "origin" of sexuality? As Laplanche and Pontalis write, sexuality is born in the virtual moment when fantasy disengages from the natural object. Or to put it another way: in losing, in veering away from the real body of the mother, the mouth remembers her in fantasy, and this remembrance inaugurates sexuality (p. 16). Fantasy and sexuality stem from the same autoerotic push: the erotic discourse that unfolds even in (because of?) the absence of the other.

The very nature of fantasy, a discourse without address, is imbricated with that strange early time in human development when the nascent subject is emerging from the mother–infant dyad. In the period before Oedipus, that is, before gender (for the child) the mother–infant bond is specular, a relationship of in-between in which the boundaries of self and other are blurred. In this amorphous field, the mouth serves as a point of intersection between local infantile pleasure and the mother's seductive presence, and at this site, memory constitutes sexuality from loss. In the ebb and flow of another's presence and the play between loss and memory, orality inscribes in sexuality the preeminent *jouissance* of the maternal body. Some lesbian personals delight in recapturing the sexuality of the mouth:

Seduction

You seduce me by inviting my eyes to your décolletage, your arms around my neck inviting my kiss, your breathing telling me not to stop. I seduce you with my strong butch touch, a shivery bite to your neck, my tongue and then my fingers in your mouth, pressing your body between mine and the wall.

Although "décolletage" has a certain Victorian sex appeal, it was the mouth that seduced me into the erotics of lesbian ads. In orality, lack is not marked by the stigma of sexual difference and the privilege of the phallus. In the mouth, genderless, I found (in) myself a part of the lesbian scene.

I felt, of course, the haunting twinge of a dusty psychoanalysis. Homosexuality, it would say, is a boy's rejection of sexual difference (castration terror rears its ugly head) and identification with the mother: orality is a throwback to a primitive, regressed, infantile world. Yet remembering orality provided a way to cross gender and reappropriate the joy of infantile sex. In *Male Subjectivity at the Margins,* Kaja Silverman demonstrates the workings of femininity at the heart of male homosexuality, and this project bears some examination here.[8] She broadens the traditional paradigm of male homosexuality beyond simple identification with the mother and desire for the father. In what she calls the "Leonardo model" of homosexuality (following Freud's "Leonardo da Vinci and a Memory of His Childhood"), she extends the oedipal scenario to a fantasy scene in which the male subject is in "constant oscillation" (p. 371) between identification with and desire for the positions of mother and (the self remembered as) child. In identifying with the mother position, the subject desires another as he himself was desired by the mother; in identifying with who he once was as a child, he desires another who structurally occupies the maternal position. The fundamental circuit of desire is based on the mother–infant dyad and a remembering subject. The implication is that difference is thus not constituted as sex (the gender difference between mother and father) but, rather, as the more complex difference between mother and infant. At its most simple, this relationship is marked by differentiation, the emergence of two bodies from one. Here, big nurtures (or tortures or abandons) little; give and take are the fundamental operations; the devourer lies in the arms of the devoured; and love (or hate) distorts the boundedness of bodies.

In explaining desire between men, Silverman's construction makes homo-sense from the perspective of maternal identification (like my mother, I love a boy [like me]), but hetero-sense from the infant's position (I want a mother).

How, then, are the vestiges of longing for the mother's body kept alive in the longing between men? Following Probyn, I want to queer the dim memory of the mother's body from the origin of a homosexual present. Let's rewind the story. The "original" maternal–child scene is hallucinatory and vague and from the shadows of the dyad slowly emerges a separate self, a new subject. The difference between the bodies crystallizes, but for the infant it is a difference not embodied by gender. It is difference more radically distilled: self, not-self; same, other. Now, from a gendered postoedipal world, I can read retroactively, to reach back and radically gender the liminal difference of infant self and maternal other. This is a difference that oscillates at the dizzy edge between being one and being two. Desire for the maternal body is a longing for sameness, for homo-ness. Traditional psychoanalytic theory and Silverman invoke a "phallic" mother to mirror the sameness of the boy. I say you can throw away the "phallic" mother: the penis-as-phallus means nothing to the preoedipal child. The mother–child dyad is lesbian.

Part of the pleasure of homo-sex is the thrill of oscillation between identification and desire: it is not just that two women, or two men, having sex are the "same"; it's that they are the same and different at the same time. Perhaps more forcefully than heterosexual or gay male eroticism, lesbian erotics echo the dangerous excitement at stake in physical ecstasy—merger, the melting of boundaries, engulfment, personal dissolution.

Lesbian erotics are obviously not reducible to a memory of mother. But as a gay man claiming this remembrance from a queer perspective, I found in the maternal body a way to identify with lesbian sex. If reading lesbian personal ads has been an exercise in finding a (re)connection with women's bodies, it has been so through my homosexuality. I know the delights of sliding between identification with and desire for the body of my lover. The want ads market of lesbian fantasy has opened a door to reconstructing infant eros from the queer present. Imagining that distant sameness between mother and child through the lens of my homosexuality has reconstructed mother–child erotics as lesbian. And this queering of memory has opened a new place of identification for me in lesbian fantasies.

Gay men could stand to learn something from lesbian sex, but there is still not much space for explicit femininity in the sexual economy of Tom of Finland. Whereas lesbians have appropriated the strap-on phallus, the bodies of women—imagistically, symbolically—are too easily elided from the fantasies of sex between men. Reading lesbian personals has given me a keyhole through which to peer into my own fantasies and thus to reconfigure them.

In sexual moments I could feel the hallucinatory pull of the maternal. The difference in size, the feeding, nurturing, holding. I felt in the body of my lover the return of a maternal gaze that said, Look, let me show who you are. In these moments, when I reconceived him in the space of that first other, I loved him as I imagine a woman loves a woman.

I began to imagine the inscriptions of lesbian sexuality in men's attraction to men.

I met an andro-fem in a bar: flannel shirt, sneakers. He told me the story of his relationship's demise, the aftermath of the last heartbreak: five years, he lost the dog, kept the mortgage. It was the cautionary tale of a marriage gone bad. He kept referring to his former partner as his "husband." I didn't think of Ward and June Cleaver: I imagined Daisy, the outboard motor, and the good wife; I thought of the lesbian couples living in Bernal Heights.

The men's personal ads took on lesbian subtexts. A sudden rash of ads looking for "Boy Pussy" seemed to confirm synergistically my new revision. In the references to "oral service" and "feeding," I read the transformation of phallic erotics into the abstracted bliss of the nipple–mouth machine. "Big Man seeks Daddy's Boy," a fellatio extravaganza, now seemed like a transgender version of mother and child.

In the streets, I started to classify my cruise by lesbian gender: soft butch bottoms and andro-fem tops, switches. A leather clone in the Castro could easily be resexed as a femmy leather queen looking for her dyke daddy.

I began to see the woman in all those hairy bears. I like it. It gets me wet.

Notes

1. Samuel R. Delany, "Sword & Sorcery, S/M, and the Economics of Inadequation: The Camera Obscura Interview," in Samuel R. Delany,

ed., *Silent Interviews* (Hanover, N.H.: Wesleyan University Press, 1994), pp. 127–163.

2. Jean Laplanche and J.-B. Pontalis, "Fantasy and the Origins of Sexuality," *International Journal of Psychoanalysis* 49 (1968): 17. In this and future references, page numbers are given in the text.

3. The list of abbreviations is extensive and range from the standard (ISO = "in search of"; SBiM = "single bisexual male"; bl/bl = "blonde hair, blue eyes") to the more specialized (VA = "verbal abuse"; B&D = "bondage and discipline"; TV = "transvestite"; NS = "nonsmoker").

4. Laura Kipnis, "(Male) Desire and (Female) Disgust: Reading Hustler," in Laura Kipnis, *Ecstasy Unlimited: On Sex, Capital, Gender, and Aesthetics* (Minneapolis: University of Minnesota Press, 1993), pp. 219–241.

5. Fashion is not glib. Is it any wonder that queer performativity was catapulted to the fore by a lesbian?

6. Teresa de Lauretis, *The Practice of Love: Lesbian Sexuality and Perverse Desire* (Bloomington: Indiana University Press, 1994), p. 96.

7. Elspeth Probyn, "Suspended Beginnings: Of Childhood and Nostalgia," *GLQ: A Journal of Lesbian and Gay Studies* 2 (1995): 439–485.

8. Kaja Silverman, *Male Subjectivity at the Margins* (New York: Routledge, 1992).

C H A  P T E R

Passage

Sandra Lee Golvin

The cock rests snugly in my pants, says tonight there is no turning back. In the dark of my mind, under cover of night, I sort through my own queerness. A femme, always. Hungry for that butch swagger, that stance of manhood, that cool dude who can handle me, contain my fire, meet it. Yes. But my body doesn't match. My body has its own boy ways. Calves too big for a girl. "Are you a dancer?" they ask from thirteen on. Until women's lib and I stop shaving. Then the real freak emerges. Thighs on down the muscled hairy legs of a man (only shorter). Start fucking girls and the beard grows, the moustache grows. Breasts not quite all there. "Looks like they've been deflated," a college roommate says. Never could walk in heels. Always felt in drag that way. But I do like to wear dresses. Especially the sweet sailor suits of a young girl.

And now, in my early forties, the boy wants to come out. But he's not interested in girls. He likes boys. Boys who like boys. Or girls who act like boys who like boys. Joan Nestle says all femmes turn butch after forty, but this isn't butch. It's something else that

I can't name. But I know what makes me hungry. And I know it is why I am here. And I could just about die from the degree and depth of dislocation this unnatural (by any definition) desire brings up in me. The horror of unrequited love.

Tonight I join one hundred dykes and fags in an invented ceremony someone has named "queer among queers." In this circle I am invited to enter the psychic place that makes me other, even among my peers, even to myself, the place of wounding, the place of silence, the place of shame. I close my eyes, safe in the dark, to find this space where I live. When I arrive, the voice of our guide reaches into the abyss to draw the boy out.

I am told there are people in the center of the room, people who have volunteered to care, people to whom they say we can each bring the story of our shame, people who will listen and understand. I am told to find the one who is right for me. I do not believe in refuge. I have lived in this body too long to trust that there will ever be a home. Yet I cannot help wanting what they say is offered, cannot help wanting to be seen for my whole freakish self, seen and embraced and loved. So I survey the people who say they will take this boy in. Those who call themselves dykes and faggots, lesbians and gay men. Those who are called queer community. Those who can hurt me most of all.

And I choose.

He is a beautiful young man. I have watched him these past few days, noticed the hot combination of man and woman in him, with his bare brown pecs, gauzy skirt over strong legs, ponytail heavy down his ropey back, black moustache and thick-lashed questioning eyes. And he is Cuban, just like my longtime butch lover. Yes, he is the one I want.

I rise to my feet and move to him. Terror accompanies my desire like a bride with her groom, a wedding of heaven and hell. My march forward is as slow as that one I never made down any church aisle. Fists balled up in the pockets of my leather jacket, the smell of my own sweat stands in for the bridal bouquet.

"Welcome my daughter," he says, drawing me up next to him. His words hit me like a punch to the stomach. How can he call me daughter? Doesn't he see who I am?

"I'm not your daughter," I whisper into his shoulder, the words barely choked up through the weight of a lifetime of silence. But he hears me.

"Oh," he says easily, "who are you, then?"

I brace myself against his disgust and reply.

"I'm your son," I hear myself say and then add. "I'm not just your son. I'm your gay son."

When he stands his ground and does not leave, my words echo back at me, rattle through my beleaguered body like a hometown quake. Hold me I pray, hold me so I don't split apart from trying to name the unnameable, from trying to be the un-be-able, from trying to find one single unified place from which to navigate this impossible world. I taste salt, the fluid of grief, the release of something held too long at bay. Yes I am crying. Letting myself be held at last.

But I don't stay long in that place before I begin to worry about him. How can he possibly understand what I am telling him when I don't understand it myself? I try to read his reaction. He seems genuinely pleased to find this gay boy in his arms. Do I dare to trust this? The energy shifts. I begin to rub my crotch against his leg. I wonder if he can feel the soft sponge dick I put in my jockey briefs when I first dressed for this evening's gathering. I push up against him, wonder if he will get hard. That change from soft to hard is the wonder I seek. When I was an adolescent I did all the boys, down on my knees, eyes closed, worshiping at the altar of that miracle. What was I then? It looked like straight sex, a boy and a girl. But now I know what I know, and though I may not be able to name my gender, the one thing that's sure is that I'm queer as a three-dollar bill. What I want tonight is that ticket to the queer place, the forbidden territory of man to man. How does a man long for another man? The hunger that burns between my legs as I imagine his hard heat doesn't feel like the hunger of other for other, but the undeniably queer desire of like to like.

But what is his vision of me? Can he think of me as I want him to, not as a woman but as someone he could want? I wish he would kiss me, open his mouth, and give me his tongue, but he doesn't. How do I read this? From what I have heard of man sex, hesitation plays no part when the dick rises to feed its cravings. Do I dare to reach down to where the appetite lives, run fingertips up along the object of desire in search of the stiffening that will tell me if I am met, bring my lips humbly to the place of my dream? I can go no further without his help, a signal of permission for crossing the line, and it does not come. There is only compassion (pity?) in his arms around me, this terrible awkward rubbing and my own strange need. How does a man long for another man? I am left waiting at the altar.

We return to the perimeter, one large circle again. Then one by one, we take our turn before the group. I watch as others seek to make the meaning of their experience understood. The multiple faces of the outsider. One person admits to bisexuality, another to the seduction of drag. Sympathy swells, clapping, shouting, tears let each speaker know he or she is heard. I take the center alone, stumble over the effort to translate this body into words. I say: "Every part of me is queer. The girl and the boy."

Is it my imagination, or is the uncomprehending silence that meets my announcement far louder than any applause that came before? My shameful effort to pass myself off as other than female ricochets back at me in the image of my stocky little boy, a hundred distorted pictures as if from a fun house of mirrors. This twisted desire, this pretender to the masculine, this thing that cannot be named. Even here among the outlaws of gender, I cannot find a place to belong.

The woman who confessed her bisexuality touches my arm when I sit back down. I am grateful for the human gesture, but I know she thinks we share the same shame. "That's not what I'm talking about," I want to tell her as my empty hands clench and unclench in the cocoon of my jacket pockets, "that's not what I'm talking about at all."

Two years later, I sit down to write this story. The phone rings. It's my guy. We haven't spoken since our meeting that night at the center of the circle. He is coming to Los Angeles, wants to get together. I tell him I'm writing about him, about that night. Does he remember? Of course, he assures me, he remembers. I'm slightly relieved. Maybe I'll send him my piece, get his reaction. But I don't.

At the West Hollywood gay-boy inn, I thread past the pool where the disco beat pumps in the late afternoon. I bang on his door. No answer. Jesus? I call, bang again. He opens the door. He is naked. I got him out of the shower. He runs back to the bathroom, finishes rinsing, then emerges to greet me. I wait for him to get dressed, but he doesn't. What's happening here? Am I supposed to make a move? It's great to see you, he tells me. You too, I say, and then I add: I didn't expect to see so much of you. I guess I've made him feel bad because now he gets dressed. I'm sorry.

I take him to dinner at Versailles, best Cuban food in town. I ask again if he remembers that night. Sure. He laughs. I tell him some of what I've written here, my embarrassment, awkwardness. What was your experience? I ask. He remembers us sort of rubbing against each other. He was letting me take the lead. Then he wants to know what I think of when I think of sex with him. Do I want to fuck or be fucked? I don't know that I've thought about it like that, I say, buying time. The specifics have always escaped me. Because, he explains, he likes to be fucked. Oh, he can do the other thing, but it doesn't take him to that place he can go when he's receiving.

That night, between us, he was ready to receive. I don't know what I wanted, I say. I like to be on my knees, I like it in the mouth. Is that the problem, I wonder aloud, all this time I've been thinking I didn't know what to do with a guy, but the problem was that we're both bottoms? We laugh.

I relax a little now; it's been settled. Our desires just don't match.

Later, after I drop him off and we hug good-bye, I remember what he said. That night. About how he was ready to receive me. Something stirs between my legs. The specificity of my hunger hits me with the truth that could never before be named. I wanted to fuck him. What line has been drawn that cannot be crossed? Boy and girl? Dyke and fag? Old and young? Oh yes, I wanted to fuck him.

It was my own power to take us there that I feared.

CHAPTER 4

The Ick Factor: Flesh, Fluids, and Cross-Gender Revulsion

Eric Rofes

I meet two lesbian friends for lunch at an outdoor café on Castro Street. After salads and sandwiches and a lengthy conversation, we walk through the neighborhood; I run into another friend and start talking. The women start necking—right on the street. Out of the corner of my eye, I see one wrap her arm around the other, pull her lover's face up to meet her own, and kiss, at first quickly and casually and then more slowly and deeply. Although I never look directly at the women, my breath begins to shorten and my stomach quivers. As they make out, I can't deny I feel a little sick.

I am at the movies watching *Personal Best* or *Go Fish,* depending on the year. I'm interested in representations of lesbians in the media, but whenever (limited) lesbian sex appears on the screen, I notice a familiar reaction. I can watch hugging and kissing with no problem, but when bodies appear naked, when hints of certain body parts (breasts and cunts), activities (cunnilingus, fingering, breast kissing or biting) or fluids (sweat, saliva) appear, I look away from the screen, feel queasy, and cautiously glance back to the film, anxiously hoping for a sudden shift in the scene.

A group of male friends and I are vacationing in Provincetown and drive to Herring Cove Beach for a day in the sun. We plan to sit in the gay guys' section but first must trudge through acres of lesbians who are reading books, playing paddle ball, or sitting in circles talking. Many have taken off the tops of their bathing suits. I'm never sure of the etiquette here: Is it OK to look directly at breasts, or is this too traditionally male? I find myself alternately grossed out and transfixed by the women. My eyes dart from the women's tits to the sand, to the tits, to their faces, to the sand. My forehead gets clammy. I see all kinds of breasts, all kinds of women's bodies—different sizes and colors, some smooth and some hairy, some dry and some sweaty. When we finally walk beyond the women's section and male torsos appear, my breath eases, my skin stops sweating, and my heart stops racing.

I am a gay man with long-term friendships with lesbians and a strong commitment to supporting lesbian culture. Yet I'm one of many gay men who share what I call "the ick factor"—a visceral response ranging from dislike to disgust when confronted with lesbian sex and bodies. Over almost twenty-five years of involvement in gay male cultures, I've witnessed many men express their revulsion at lesbian sex and women's bodies. I've heard countless "tuna" jokes, seen men's faces turn sour when lesbian sex appears in movies, and watched gay men huddle together in small groups voicing disgust at topless women in political demonstrations. Recently when a sexualized, naked woman appeared on-screen in a gay male porn flick showing in the Castro, men started hooting and yelling "fish" comments. The man in front of me turned to his friend and whispered loudly, "Gross me out!"

Though often unacknowledged and unexamined, the ick factor may be at the heart of many gay men's inability to take women seriously, support lesbian concerns, or develop meaningful relationships with women. By examining the ick factor in this essay, I hope to grapple with some of the key barriers that keep gay men from deeper relationships with lesbians and gain a greater understanding of some of the ways in which an array of social and cultural power dynamics become mapped onto the body, its activities, and its functions.

Although I can recall "icky" feelings about girls' and women's bodies since my childhood, it was only recently that I began to confront them directly. For the last five years, a lesbian friend and colleague and I have convened a workshop called "The Ick Factor" at the National Gay and Lesbian Task Force's annual Creating Change conference.[1] The workshop was conceived as an opportunity for lesbians and gay men to talk about sex across gender lines and to discuss all kinds of cross-gender curiosity and revulsion. It opened my eyes to the wide range of responses that lesbians and gay men have to each other's sexualities, sexual practices, and sex cultures. It also provided me with numerous opportunities to talk with other gay men about the ick factor, to learn about their experiences and thoughts, and to begin to work through some of these things.

The workshop is often standing room only, with women and men packed together in a hotel meeting room, sitting braced with anticipation. Over the years, a range of perspectives have surfaced during these discussions, but the workshop has always been a place where gay men have been able to examine publicly their "ick." One year a man talked at length about his becoming nauseated at the idea of two lesbians "eating each other out," yet he seemed obsessed with describing the event he supposedly found revolting. Another spoke about his inability to become physically close to lesbians because of the odors he believed their bodies emitted. Once a gay man confessed to me after the workshop that he enjoyed having sex with lesbians as long as he could avoid their genitals, which made him ill. As he talked about being fucked by women wearing strap-on dildos or anally penetrating lesbians, I detected a mixture of excitement and disgust in his voice, which pretty much matched my own feelings.

I've come to believe that gay men can be divided into three groups, of approximately the same size: those who find the lesbian body erotic, those who have no feelings about it at all, and those who experience "the ick." Many gay men appreciate women's bodies and experience no feelings of disgust when confronted with lesbian sex. Some find women's bodies sexually attractive, and a few men who spoke at the conference workshop confessed to being turned on to women's having sex with women. Still other gay-identified men enjoy sex with women (including women who identify themselves as lesbians), raising familiar debates about bisexual identity and practice. Yet significant numbers of gay men at the workshops and outside, in the social worlds I inhabit, have talked about experiencing some kind of "ick," although their particular triggers for revulsion and responses to specific sexual acts fit no single pattern.

Conversations with lesbians have led me to believe that even though some lesbians share a parallel range of ick responses, the sources of their ick and the sociopolitical issues surrounding it may be different. Many lesbians explain their disgust with penises, sperm, man-to-man rimming and fisting, and other activities as rooted in their experiences of violence, rape, incest, and childhood sexual assault perpetrated by men or boys. In the five years that I participated in open discussions on this topic at queer conferences, not a single gay man attributed his ick factor to violence perpetrated by women or girls.

Gay Men and Lesbian Sex

Lesbians are constantly confronted with issues, images, and experiences focused on gay male sexuality. Most lesbian and gay periodicals contain pages filled with graphic advertisements marketing gay phone-sex lines, hustlers and masseurs, sex toys, festivals, and cruises. Marches on Washington and pride parades teem with brazenly sexual men—ranging from muscle-boy clones who gleefully rip off their shirts at the drop of a hat; to leather men in harnesses, dog collars, and leashes; to a range of community groups (ranging from Black and White Men Together to the Bear clubs) organized around specific erotic fetishism.

Yet most gay men rarely see, hear about, or politically confront anything having to do with lesbian sex. In fact, the many gay men who have no lesbian friends, do not go to the few lesbian films that appear in movie houses, and don't read lesbian-focused publications may never formally confront lesbians as sexual beings at all.

Annual lesbian and gay pride parades, "dyke marches," and the infrequent gay and lesbian marches on Washington have become primary sites for gay men's confrontation with women's bodies and lesbian sexuality. The responses to bare-breasted lesbians, bawdy dyke humor, and public representations of lesbian sex, though diverse and uneven, occur primarily through informal channels—comments and asides in all-male settings or grumbling in the ranks of march organizing committees. Such responses occasionally find their way into America's "queer public sphere"—the letters to the editor pages of the gay press—and increasingly into the mainstream media.[2]

Boston's pride parade in 1996 evoked such a response. What one newspaper described as "a guerrilla theater rolling bed on which topless women simulated sex"[3] ignited a firestorm of debate in the days following the parade, including a lead editorial in the local gay paper entitled "Gross Stupidity at a Great Parade."[4] The gay male editor of that local gay paper claimed he'd "received more angry phone calls and letters—from conservatives and progressives—regarding these incidents than any other event in the last eight years." Nonetheless, for three sentences, his editorial focused on an unidentified male flasher (dismissed as "an aberration" who "forgot his medication"), and for three vitriolic paragraphs, he concentrated on the Lesbian Avengers who staged the acts on the moving bed. At a town meeting to discuss the controversy, a member of the dyke march committee astutely stated:

> It's interesting that the year that the lesbians decided to be relatively sexual, out in the open, there's been so much controversy. And yet for years upon years men have been humping each other without a whimper or cry being heard from the public. If this isn't blatant sexism, I don't know what is.[5]

Blatant sexism, yes, but I argue that the level of outrage concerning this incident illustrates a dynamic more complex than simple sexism. A gay Republican activist dubbed the act "extreme behavior" and "unhelpful, dumb, and silly," and a local gay male activist decried the "small group of obnoxious women pushing a bed in the parade, with their only goal to offend" and insisted that the "jerk on stilts who kept exposing himself" was "not as offensive" as the lesbians who simply simulated sexual behavior and did not expose their genitals.

I have rarely seen sexualized gay male interactions at pride events or marches on Washington described in such terms except in far-right propaganda videotapes. But gay male sexuality in public spaces is more common than lesbian sexuality in public spaces. During pride marches and festivals, it's common to see men dancing together, with one's chest against the other's back, crotch against butt, in acts of simulated butt fucking. When I have witnessed such spectacles—and when I have participated in them myself—they have been considered wild or risqué, celebrations of male erotic energy, freedom, and love. I have never heard critical comments from lesbians or gay men or seen letters to the editor in gay newspapers following such activities.

At the core, this observation is about much more than a sexist distinction between who gets away with performing antics and who doesn't. It is about the revulsion many gay men feel at the sight of women's breasts, women eating each other out, and women as self-defined sexual beings and the tremendous threat this poses to the patriarchal status quo. It's about many men's power, access, and resources to channel that revulsion and fear into newspaper text, punitive legal responses, and political action.

Theorizing Revulsion

As social practice, revulsion is commonly considered to be a physiological response triggered by a particular causative agent, almost in the way that an allergy is triggered by a specific allergen. I might explain that witnessing medical operations "makes me sick" or that the sight of blood causes me to faint.

When specific sexual practices are identified as evoking revulsion, we articulate this response as a matter of "taste" and frequently probe no further. The French social theorist Pierre Bourdieu suggests that disgust merits deconstruction and that what many naturalize as "good taste" emerges out of powerful social, economic, and cultural processes.

> Tastes (i.e., manifested preferences) are the practical affirmation of an inevitable difference. It is no accident that, when they have to be justified, they are asserted purely negatively, by the refusal of other tastes. In matters of taste, more than anywhere else, all determination is negation, and tastes are perhaps first and foremost distastes, disgust provoked by horror or visceral intolerance ("sick-making") of the tastes of others. . . . Aesthetic intolerance can be terribly violent.

When gay men are confronted with the assumption that our homosexuality is rooted in our dislike for women, we often answer that male homosexuality has nothing to do with women—it's about loving men. Our reaction to women's bodies, however, suggests otherwise. An image of a single, naked female body with exposed breasts and genitals may simultaneously fascinate and repulse me. Add a second female nude and make the image sexual (cunnilingus, for example, or even simply kissing), and my revulsion intensifies while the fascination wanes. But make this an image of a naked female and a naked man engaged in some sexual activity, and the revulsion subsides significantly and the fascination increases.

Does the addition of a body that's gendered male distract my gaze and hence diminish the ick? Or does the disgust ease because the presence of a man frames female body parts in more traditional ways that appear less upsetting to me? Might my disgust simply be a historically rooted resistance to the centerfold nudies pushed before my face as I huddled in dark corners with boyhood friends? Or is there something threatening about naked, sexualized images of women's bodies that are not in a discursive relationship to male bodies?

Of course, my fear and disgust with women's bodies may also be the way I channel a larger fear of sex, of male bodies, of my own holes and fluids. It seems easier to project revulsion onto the female than to confront it in relation to the male. At sex clubs, I might gaze in horror and fascination at a male forearm protruding from a man's ass, but there are no spaces in which I verbalize that disgust. Perhaps the implication of this revulsion for my identity is more than I can handle.

Male homosexuality and gay male identity might be best understood as terms that simplistically reduce a variety of complex constructions of masculinity and strategies of sexual/social practice to one common term. Searches for "the cause" of homosexuality may be misguided not only because they biologize, geneticize, or psychologize identities that are socially and culturally constructed but also because they draw together, unite, and reduce practices that are distinct and independently generated. Perhaps the only commonality among homosexualities as social practices is that the term has come to signify the presence of erotic relations focused on one's own gender and the absence of relations with the other gender.

Bourdieu's insistence that all determination is negation and all tastes are distastes raises a number of questions about categories and classifications of sexual "preference." Is monosexuality as evidenced in the practices of heterosexuality and homosexuality an aesthetic of intolerance? Does my comfort in an arm gendered male, a face marked with a beard, and genitalia containing dick and balls contain negation? When Bourdieu writes that "taste is what brings together things and people that go together" (p. 241), might he mean that a disgust for cunt draws men together into a gay community?[6] Do heterosexual and homosexual men share in misogyny, with one group disgusted by cunts and the other feeling (mostly) attraction? Is the only difference between heterosexual men and homosexual men the body part chosen as object of visceral horror?

> The sense of distinction, the *discretio* (discrimination) which demands that certain things be brought together and others kept apart, which excludes all misalliances and all unnatural unions—i.e., all unions contrary to the common classification, the *diacrisis* (separation) which is the basis of collective and individual identity—responds with visceral, murderous horror, absolute disgust, metaphysical fury, to everything which lies in Plato's "hybrid zone," everything which passes understanding, that is, the embodied taxonomy, which, by challenging the principles of the incarnate social order, especially the socially constituted principles of the sexual division of labour and the division of sexual labour, violates the mental order, scandalously flouting common sense.[7]

Perhaps disgust itself is a social practice that serves to draw a line around a population and hold it separate from others. Could my revulsion at lesbian sex function as an everyday practice of naming myself a homosexual to myself and others? When gay men tell "fish jokes," are we engaged in a process of alliance building, hierarchization, and communal classification constructed around a gendered sexual orientation?

Sister/Woman/Sister and Endless Waterfalls

When people argue that disgust at female sexuality is inextricably linked to misogyny, I immediately want to argue otherwise.

Yet I have come to believe the ick factor is impervious to ideology; it's so deeply inscribed in some men's bodies and minds that a dose or two of feminism has little impact. My own experience offers clues to why the ick factor has implications beyond everyday social practice and why, despite being steeped in feminism and inculcated in antisexist politics, disgust with women's sexuality may persist in gay men.

I came out as a gay man during the 1970s. While my social life was primarily situated in sexualized gay male spaces of the period (discos, bars, and sex clubs), my political life was based in the *Gay Community News* collective, a leftist, cogender group of activists/journalists that was a site of self-conscious struggle and debate about gender, race, and class. My alliances with lesbians at the newspaper and my emerging commitment to cogender community brought me into close contact with Boston's burgeoning women's culture of that period.

For a decade, I regularly attended women's music concerts, feminist bookstores, and activist events focused on women's issues. I eagerly awaited books published by feminist presses, read women's newspapers and feminist theory, and volunteered to provide child care at lesbian cultural events and a local shelter for battered women. My stereo played records ranging from early Village People to Alix Dobkin, Mary Watkins, and Meg Christian. Lyrics from Holly Near's *Sister/Woman/Sister* might filter through my head during a trip to the Mineshaft. For a while, my favorite background music for sex was Cris Williamson's *Waterfall,* with its powerful woman-centered erotic lyrics about "filling up" and "spilling over."

For a brief time, I regarded myself as one of the gay male "lesbian wannabes" of this period, a small subculture of gay men who developed a deep envy of lesbian–feminist culture. We wore loose-fitting shirts, drawstring pants, and Birkenstocks. We tried to produce male counterparts to the evolving women's culture: men's music albums, men's rural gatherings, resource centers for "changing men." Yet our efforts had limited appeal to most gay men, who were busily engaged in building sexualized urban cultures of highly charged, hypermasculine images. My immersion in gay male sex cultures of the period—and particularly the men's-only leather scene on the East Coast—soon moderated any lesbian envy I may have felt. What does it mean that a key cultural thread weaving its way through my emerging identity was "womyn centered"? How did this relate to my queasiness around women's bodies and my emerging awareness of my visceral distaste for women's sexuality? I could spend hours flipping through the catalog for Judy Chicago's *The Dinner Party,* admiring the vaginal imagery central to each place setting, but the thought of real-live cunt would turn my stomach. I'd sixty-nine my boyfriend while Cris Williamson's *Waterfall* would fill up and spill over, but walking in on lesbian roommates engaged in cunnilingus would make me become faint and I'd have to lie down.

Except on rare, awkward occasions, my tour through women's cultures of the period did not powerfully confront me with women's sexuality. In retrospect, the sites and texts I was able to access—women's music concerts, activist publications, feminist poetry and novels—privileged a lesbian–feminist political culture that de-emphasized the explicitly sexual. I'd see women holding hands and hugging, hear song lyrics that only obliquely referenced the erotic, and read lesbian fiction that, with rare exceptions, provided a romanticized and sanitized vision of sex between women. Before the lesbian sex wars raged and challenged hegemonic utopian visions of sexuality in women's culture, the vision of women's culture I witnessed (overwhelmingly white, middle class, and Protestant) was dominated by "womyn-loving-womyn" and was rarely troubled by matters such as dildos, handcuffs, power exchanges, or promiscuity.[8]

In contrast, I recall directly confronting women's bodies and sexuality when a dyke couple visited my small, summer rental in Provincetown as weekend houseguests. The women seemed to spend hours lolling around naked, entwined on the floor of the small shower, or walking around the apartment topless. I felt queasy.

That hot summer, it seemed fair for friends of any gender to be as comfortable as they'd like in the privacy of my steamy, un-air-conditioned home. Yet why didn't it also seem fair for me to express my visceral reaction? The fragile linkages between lesbians and gay men during this period made me cautious—few relationships of the time seemed to survive intellectual disagreement, social offenses, or political errors.

Perhaps more significantly, my own discomfort with my body at the time did not allow me to express myself easily—I rarely went shirtless, even at home. During these years when gay (white) men were constructing idealized visions of "the gay (white) body" in gay ghetto gyms throughout the nation, I think much of my disgust at women's breasts and nipples must have intersected with my conflict about my own place in the emerging "pec culture" of the times.

On one especially warm afternoon, I bicycled to the beach and my friends went onto the porch of the apartment. On returning, I was met by an angry gay male neighbor, insisting I'd scandalized the neighborhood by permitting my guests to go topless in public. He told me that he'd had to retreat indoors, explaining that the women were "making out" and "going at it" in full view of all. He'd complained to my landlady, who lived in the next building and who had expressed similar concerns.

I recall reacting in an extreme manner—chastising my friends, shaming them, insisting they'd selfishly failed to consider the implications of their nudity on the remainder of my summer. On thinking back to the incident, I'm struck by how much of my response was about my neighborhood relations and how much was about my own revulsion at their bodies. Would my responses have been similar had two men been caught "going at it" on the back porch? Or was an undercurrent of disgust, outrage, and fury over women's bodies the engine behind my response?

The Centrality of Cunt to Gay Men's Sex

As Peter Stallybrass and Allon White wrote, "What is *socially* peripheral is so frequently *symbolically* central."[9] What do I make of the nexus between my revulsion at women's bodies and genitals and the predilection of many gay men, including myself, to refer to the male orifices that we enter as *pussies* and *cunts?* If the ubiquitous "no fems" is attached to gay male personal ads to keep femininity at a distance, why do so many other ads seek "tits and ass," "big nipples," "smooth holes," "pussy throats," and men with "large, sloppy cunts?"[10] Perhaps we're seeing what Stallybrass and White consider "a perfect representation of the production of identity through negation, the creation of an implicit sense of self through explicit rejections and denials" (p. 89).

When a "bear" I meet on the street takes me back to his apartment, starts sitting on my face, and tells me, "Lick my hole, kid. Taste that hairy cunt. Chew on that pussy," I bury my own face in his tangled mane of thick hairs, and suck and lick with great delight. Why is his "cunt" wonderful to me, when women's cunts are revolting? If terms such as *pussy* inspire revulsion in some gay men, why do we inject them into our sex?

According to Bourdieu,

> Disgust is the paradoxical experience of enjoyment extorted by violence, an enjoyment which arouses horror. This horror, unknown to those who surrender to sensation, results fundamentally from removal of the distance, in which freedom is asserted, between the representation and the thing represented, in short from alienation, the loss of the subject in the object, immediate submission to the immediate present under the enslaving violence of the "agreeable."[11]

Is the horror I feel reading the sexually graphic parts of lesbian poetry or fiction actually an "enjoyment extorted by violence?" Does the ick that I feel in relation to women's bodies simply serve to mask deeply held forbidden pleasures, obsessive delights, from which the acquisition of gay male identity has severed me? Are all gay men truly bisexual or polysexual beings—or only those of us whose desires have been twisted and contorted into an ick? Some have suggested that our erotic lives are the sites where we wrestle with the deeper tensions in our lives and where we attempt to resolve vexing conflicts and disentangle the twists and kinks of our psyches. Hearing men spit into public urinals makes me ill; swapping spit with a sex partner exhilarates and excites me. Perhaps the centrality of cunt in my own homo-sex life suggests that the flip side of disgust may be desire.

Implications for a Cogender Movement

Most men seem to be unable to deeply empathize, support, or understand a range of women's health, economic, and sociopolitical issues. At different times, some of us have described the barrier as the obsessive self-centeredness of patriarchy, men's inability to see beyond themselves, or the drain of AIDS on gay men's energies.[12] Some lesbian activists have explained men's consistent failure to "deliver the goods" for women (equity of funding, services, or power) as examples of sexism and misogyny.

Of course, gay men have often spoken out in public settings to applaud "the lesbians" for their selfless support for gay men amid the escalating AIDS crisis. This rhetoric suggests that lesbians have traditionally been the caregivers to the world and have instinctively dropped other commitments (and outstanding grievances) to care for their "brothers" facing the plague. Gay men usually close such speeches with a commitment to support women facing "the epidemic of breast cancer," which is followed by thunderous applause and a standing ovation.

I am waiting for the time when lesbian activists respond to this by silently rising and turning their backs. Gay men have not gotten significantly involved in the fight against breast cancer—or in any of the dozens of health issues confronting their lesbian "sisters."[13] Men rarely contribute much money or volunteer hours to women's health organizations, provide individual support services to ill lesbians, or make the effort to acquire even a superficial knowledge of women's health issues.

For some gay men, the barrier to supporting a lesbian-focused agenda may be symbolized, even naturalized, in the ick factor. What does it mean for the gay male director of a lesbian and gay community services center to be grossed out by lesbian sexual activity? Is this revulsion implicated in his failure to provide significant resources to lesbian gynecological services? How does the gay male board member of a national lesbian and gay political organization cope with his aversion to women's body smells? Does this disgust have anything to do with the failure of his group to take the lead on lesbian health advocacy or abortion rights work?[14] Is it possible for an entire range of cross-gender revulsions to circulate between gay men and lesbians without being implicated in the continuing disparity between the priority given to gay and lesbian matters in queer organizational life?

To answer these questions, we need to understand how the lesbian body has been constructed in queer social formations. As Stallybrass and White write, "The body is neither purely natural nor is it merely textual metaphor, it is a privileged metaphor for transcoding other [aspects of social life]."[15] For some gay men, a range of anxieties and social misgivings become deeply connected with and assigned to women's bodies, female functions like menstruation and childbirth and female sexual acts. A process of devaluation, denigration, and stigmatization ensues, and these bodies and their functions become objects of gay males' visceral disgust.[16]

I cannot say that the ick factor in my life bears no relationship to misogyny, as woman hating is deeply inscribed on men. Many progressive gay men may have significantly altered our social practices and established strong relationships with women, so that we do not overtly "hate" women. But our political decisions and alliances may have diverted misogyny into visceral triggers, bodily gestures, and sensory reactions to the sights, smells, and tastes gendered "female" or perceived as "dyke." I've come to believe, however, that there's more to ick than misogyny.

I am left wondering about other possibilities and questions but find few definitive answers. Are my disgust and fear of lesbian sexuality in any way a substitute for my misgivings about my own sexuality? While I maintain a sexual consciousness that on the surface holds gay male bodies, desires, and sexual practices in high esteem, do I actually hold unacknowledged revulsions to male sex?

My ick factor, after all, is not limited to women's bodies, even if I pretend that it is. I have my own set of fears about men's fluids, body parts, and sexual acts that lurk just under the surface of consciousness.

There is a great deal about gay men's sex that frightens, disgusts, and confuses me, and I do not believe I am isolated among gay men in harboring these unaddressed feelings. I wonder whether projecting these fears and revulsions onto lesbian sex offers the opportunity to project externally uncomfortable and perplexing responses that are too frightening to confront.

In this way, gay men might be doing precisely the transcoding that Stallybrass and White suggest. We transcode uncomfortable aspects of male identities and social and sexual practices onto women's bodies and sexualities. To what extent is the lesbian body forced to carry the burden of gay male fears and misgivings about our own sex? To what extent is the ick factor the social practice that inscribes these difficult-to-resolve gay male conflicts on lesbian sex?

Interrogating the ick factor offers us the possibility of learning more about ourselves as we learn more about one another. We might find that our identities as gay men are constructed on a defensive disgust at women's bodies. Or we may find that without the ick factor, our desires for other men remain solidly in place. I don't expect to find easy answers to my questions, but I do know one thing: by remaining silent about cross-gender revulsions, we allow to remain in place a entire series of body relations and social practices that divide men from women, gay man from lesbian. This is slippery ground on which to construct a movement for social change.

Notes

1. Urvashi Vaid, then the executive director of NGLTF, and Sue Hyde, the conference coordinator, conceptualized and named this workshop; I appreciate their invitation to convene it with them.

2. See, for example, Michael Greene, "Destructive Agenda," letter to the editor, *Bay Windows* (Boston), June 27, 1996, p. 7. Also see Jonathan F. Alex, "Gay Pride March Should Have Made a More Positive Statement," letter to the editor, *New York Times*, July 6, 1996.

3. "Pride and Parades," editorial, *Boston Globe*, June 15, 1996.

4. Jeff Epperly, "Gross Stupidity at a Great Parade," editorial, *Bay Windows* (Boston), June 13, 1996, p. 6.

5. Rachel Keegan, "Controversy over Pride: Whose Community Is It," *Sojourner* (Boston), July 1996, p. 18.

6. Pierre Bourdieu, *Distinction: A Social Critique of the Judgement of Taste*, trans. Richard Nice (Cambridge, Mass.: Harvard University Press, 1984), p. 56.

7. Ibid., p. 495.

8. One rare exception I recall was Kate Millet's *Sita* (New York: Ballantine Books, 1976), which at the time struck me as radically sexy. Reading it in the 1990s still excites me, yet now these passages seem heavily romanticized and a bit tame. For discussions of the de-sexing of the lesbian–feminist cultures of the 1970s and early 1980s, see Gayle Rubin, "Thinking Sex: Notes for a Radical Theory of the Politics of Sexuality," and Amber Hollibaugh, "Desire for the Future: Radical Hope in Passion and Pleasure," both in Carole S. Vance, ed., *Pleasure and Danger: Exploring Female Sexuality* (Boston: Routledge, 1984). Also see Lisa Duggan and Nan D. Hunter, *Sex Wars: Sexual Dissent and Political Culture* (New York: Routledge, 1995).

9. Peter Stallybrass and Allon White, *The Politics and Poetics of Transgression* (Ithaca, N.Y.: Cornell University Press, 1986), p. 5 (italics in original/italics added).

10. These terms, and similar phrases, were found in personal ads in various issues of *Drummer, San Francisco Sentinel,* and *Odyssey,* gay men's magazines.

11. Bourdieu, *Distinction,* p. 488.

12. One example appears in a letter to the editor in a lesbian/gay paper urging men to support Camp Sister Spirit, the Mississippi femi-

nist retreat under attack in 1993–1995. See Jay Davidson, "Support Camp Sister Spirit," *Bay Times* (San Francisco), January 27, 1994, p. 13.

13. See my discussion of this matter in Eric Rofes, *Reviving the Tribe: Regenerating Gay Men's Sexuality and Culture in the Ongoing Epidemic* (Binghamton, N.Y.: Haworth Press, 1996), pp. 258–259.

14. One notable exception was the late Ken Dawson who, in March 1992, headed the "Brothers for Sisters" campaign to raise money for Astraea, the National Lesbian Action Foundation.

15. Stallybrass and White, *Politics and Poetics,* p. 192.

16. This paragraph is heavily influenced by the work of my Berkeley colleague Matt Wray, a doctoral student in ethnic studies, and adapts portions of his paper "Unsettling Sexualities and White Trash Bodies," presented at the UC Berkeley American Studies meeting on October 10, 1994. I am grateful for his permission to paraphrase and apply his work on white trash bodies to lesbian bodies.

CHAPTER 5

In Goldilocks's Footsteps: Exploring the Discursive Construction of Gay Masculinity in Bear Magazines

Elizabeth A. Kelly and Kate Kane

> El hombre es como el oso:
> mientras más feo más hermoso [1]
>
> —*(Colombian saying)*

We Come upon This Project

Maybe it begins like the fairy tale in which once upon a time Goldilocks finds herself an uninvited guest at the home of the three bears. Or maybe it begins over coffee in a Chicago cybercafé when a friend of Beth's describes *Opposite Sex* and mentions that the editors are looking for a lesbian take on "bears"—a category of gay male sexuality that Beth's never heard of and is astonished to hear described. Within minutes, she is watching him pull various bear publications off the porn rack at the back of the lesbian and gay bookstore. Images of large, hairy, preponderantly white, male bodies—mostly naked, some playing with penises (their own or other men's) materialize before her eyes.

At first glance, these images are both fascinating and repulsive. Beth has always thought that the tyranny of slenderness was even more inscribed in gay male culture than in the normative "femininity" of compulsory heterosexuality to which she was thoroughly and oppressively socialized as a young girl and adolescent in the 1950s and 1960s and that she has spent most of her adult life resisting. It fascinates her to see bulky bodies idealized as objects of gay male desire instead of the slender, buff Adonis types she would have expected. The depictions also repel: she finds problematic the naked male bodies, however hairy/smooth or heavy/slender, even when only seen in photographs and not in the flesh.[2] Later that evening, after the first flush of scholarly enthusiasm has worn off, Beth realizes she doesn't want to write this article alone. On the one hand, she wonders whether there might be connections between the bears and the "alternative public spheres" and "intentional communities" she has written about elsewhere.[3] But on the other hand, she worries about the implications of being a lone, uninvited guest setting off to explore the bears. So she calls on Kate, a colleague who teaches the graduate course "Representations of the Body" and is not squeamish about naked men.

Kate's theoretical interests focus on bodies, boundaries, and categories. She has a friend who is a self-identified bear. An assignment to analyze gay bodies honored, valued, and desired for their largeness has great appeal to her. She immediately begins to explore the genre by quizzing her male colleagues at a lesbian and gay faculty potluck. She learns that the bear is not only a phenotype that deviates from the slender, smooth, altogether buff ideal of straight advertising and gay porn. Most of the colleagues she questions are "regular-guy" types, but all of them know of bears, and her queries evoke an assortment of definitions and responses. The gym queen recoils in horror: "Fat, hairy slobs!" Most of the men acknowledge an acquaintance with the type but disavow any personal connections to bear culture. A postlatent bear nods, "Ah, you mean the sociocultural minority of large, hairy men." There is consensus that a bear is defined by size ("a certain fleshiness") and hirsutism but less agreement on other factors such as height and age.

We learn that bears emerged as a gay male subculture in the early 1980s with a variety of forms of cultural expression, including bear bars, "clean and sober" social clubs, party weekends, conventions, and camping trips. A range of publications from porn magazines to compilations of personal ads, all focusing on bear culture in general or specific aspects of it, are available. Magazines such as *Bear* and *American Bear* feature photo spreads of large men—most of whom are tattooed, bearded, and/or noticeably hairy—along with fiction, feature articles, and an impressive array of personal ads, often accompanied by photographs. Other publications cater to even more specialized interests. *Daddybear* focuses on intergenerational sexual relations between "daddy bears" and "bear cubs"; *Heavy Duty,* as the name implies, caters to those who desire large men; and *CR (Chiron*

Rising Magazine) bills itself as offering "maturity with class" and features lots of gray- or white-haired men, intergenerational couples, and, unlike any of the others, ads for Sun Belt real estate firms and investment counselors. Although the age, hair, decorations, and size of the male bodies featured in these publications vary widely, the men depicted in the photographs and line drawings are almost exclusively white.

Kate's passion for names leads her to investigate the terminology used by gay men to mark their objects of desire. These are not unproblematic categories: a man who likes Asian men is a "rice queen"; one who admires Latinos is known variously as a "taco," "bean," "salsa," or "chili" queen; one who likes Caucasians is a "mayonnaise queen." In bell hooks's terms, this might be considered "eating the Others."[4] Kate muses about what to call a man who lusts after large hairy men—a "ranger" or a "honey queen?" Could one refer to a short bear as a "Boo-Boo?"[5] Kate's bear friend advises her to keep her silly pop-culture metaphors to herself. But Kate will not give up on one point: the bear is an interesting category in part because it designates a desiring subject and not only the object of lust.

A month goes by. Meanwhile, a package of bear magazines has arrived from San Francisco. On a warm midsummer afternoon, we meet. Kate has insisted that Beth not open the package unless both of us can be present. We decide to tape-record our reactions and conversation, in hopes that the discussion can serve as a point of reference for future analysis. The plain brown wrapper is removed with great ceremony. Nervous laughter and some fascinated perusal of images and texts ensue. At times, more than a little confusion reigns.

Kate: I'm noticing that not all the penises in these pictures are erect.

Beth: That rather escaped me—

Kate: I think they're NOT—

Beth: Well, is this erect? (pointing to an image) You know, it's been so long since I've seen one that I don't think I'd know an erect penis if I fell over one.

Kate: I don't think it is [erect].

Beth: Well, who could we call?

Eventually a few vague glimmers of thematization and analysis begin to emerge:

Kate: I wasn't sure if there was anything to this beyond the shopping-mall theory of attraction; you were thinking that there might be something resistant going on.

Beth: It seems to me that there might be a reading of this literature that draws on themes of resisting the commodification of the body and the commodification of sex. One thing that strikes me is that these are real people—these aren't gorgeous models.

Kate: Yes, I do think we might be able to say something about these being grassroots-organized expressions of desire. This isn't unique to beardom; it's found in many marginalized sexual groups.

Beth: Still, why would you want to hang your penis through a macramé hammock? Never having had a penis, this is hard for me to imagine.

Many of the photographs in the magazines we examined depict bodies and settings that are a far cry from the glossy techno-porn with the cold hard edges, huge erect dicks, and unattainable models gazing up and beyond the viewer that we usually associate with gay male iconography. There is a warm, fuzzy, countrified (if not nostalgic) quality to many of the images—hammocks, wagon wheels, flannel shirts, denim, woodsy settings.[6] Care and concern for others suffuse the verbal text accompanying bear iconography. A "Legal Perspectives" column in *Bear* discussing "Assault, Battery, and Spousal Abuse" came as a surprise. With a few pronouns and referents changed, it could easily have been found in an early edition of *MS* magazine.[7] In a 1990 column, "Bear Pause: Hug Your Teddy," the ethic of care becomes explicit when the author recalls jerking off to a picture of John Matuszak (a "big, furry, friendly, and sexy" image) in his then-wife's copy of *Playgirl* magazine. This memory surfaces in the wake of Matuszak's death from a drug overdose, and the comment is simple: "Bears don't let bears die from drugs. We help each other out, but not like that. How sad."[8]

It seems clear that a process of "reembodiment" is at work; a new discourse of gender and sexuality emerges from the texts before us. But it also seems to us that although sex and gender are focal points, the iconographies, articles, personal advertisements, trade ads, and fiction in the publications we examined presage the emergence of an alternative public sphere in which the textual configurations of sexuality and sociability are not merely articulated but enacted in ways that may be lending new meaning to the lives of the gay men who participate.

The bear "public sphere" is a fluid admixture of gay social and cultural practices—some established, such as bars, and some newly created or rediscovered, ranging from cybersex and online networking through two-step and country line-dance clubs to clean and sober barbecues, cruises, or day trips to the zoo. A description of "Great Lakes Bear Pride," a Memorial Day weekend gathering of a thousand gay men at a Chicago hotel, includes Ferris wheel rides on Navy Pier and picnicking at a lakefront park, along with notes on the "Mr. Bear Pride" competition, hot sex parties, nipple piercing, and a raffle that netted more than $3,000 to benefit local queer charities.[9] At times, out-front sexuality seems to blend with out-front political rhetoric in bear publications. For example, an interview with Mr. International Bear 1996 includes an exhortation to activism and solidarity:

> The price for segregating ourselves is turning the country over to the Christian Coalition. There are a lot of people out there in "straight" society that choose to hate us simply because of who we love. If we don't come together as a community, the entire gay community, they are going to continue to do the bad stuff to us. . . . People need to get out there and register to vote, volunteer, and make a statement for themselves.[10]

If all this can be taken at face value, then perhaps bear cultural spaces provide a point of entry into the task of reconfiguring the sort of "democratic public spheres" theorized by Jürgen Habermas and others.[11]

It's not just the public sphere with its political possibilities that we notice, however. Beth confesses (with appropriate embarrassment) that she has long been an avid reader of short stories in "women's magazines"—*Good Housekeeping, Ladies' Home Journal,* and the like.[12] She is as struck by the similarities between formula fiction for straight women and the formula fiction found in *Bear* and *American Bear* as she is by the differences. Whereas phrases such as "Daddy's boy's a good cocksucker" or "There's nothing like the taste of a cigar-smokin' man who's had his dick up your ass" will never appear in the pages of *Good Housekeeping,* romantic denouements on the order of "He folds me into an embrace, a long, strong sweetness. We both are trembling" certainly have.[13]

The personal ads in bear publications sometimes seem reminiscent of aspects of mid-1970s lesbian sexual expression. An "attractive loving gay man bottom cub . . . seeks attractive masculine sexually aggressive gay white/hispanic/black man. . . . *I am looking for a top man who is gentle enough to cuddle*" (emphasis added). We wonder whether twenty years ago this would have made it to the printed page of most gay male publications. Another example is from a couple of men who are "regular Joes, living in the real world, not gay bars, and pretty much at ease with ourselves, innocent, devilish, honest, twisted, cuddly, kissable, hungry, eager to please, and be pleased." Change "Joe" to "Jane" and this could have been placed by many generic lesbian-feminists in 1976, ourselves included.[14]

The rhetoric is not, however, vanilla. Not by a long shot. There is also raunch—lots of body smells and body fluids, from sweat to semen, and everything in between. Some of the language seems straight out of *Home Improvement* or *Coach,* or any television sitcom that makes fun of the hypermasculine space where "manly men" want to belch and head for the woods and drink beer; the "manly man" likes the smell of "manly sweat" and "manly shit" and other "manly" secretions. Yet in contrast to the impenetrable hard body of the model clone "type" of gay masculinity that emerged in the 1970s, the bear's fleshy self is not threatened by penetration, humor, or tenderness.[15]

Moreover, in his very flesh, the bear is grounded in a dual materiality: besides the large present, there are also historical precedents. Many relate the popularity of bears to AIDS and the fear of emaciated bodies as signifying illness. We see a more complex dynamic at work, however. Similar to the way in which AIDS has debilitated and decimated gay male populations in the United States for nearly twenty years, in the mid-nineteenth century, tuberculosis raged in epidemic proportions. It affected both sexes, but young women were particularly vulnerable and often died at twice the rate of men in the same age group. Of one hundred women aged twenty in 1865, more than five would die of tuberculosis before reaching thirty, and nearly ten more would die of it before reaching fifty.[16] Everyone knew someone who suffered from the disease; unlike other epidemic illnesses, it was a constant presence in everyday life. Those who contracted tuberculosis faced—and everybody feared—a lengthy illness and a slow death.[17]

In the mid-nineteenth century, epidemic tuberculosis may literally have been embodied in women who attempted to triumph over fears of infection by affecting its symptoms—the fashionable female body of the day was slender, fragile, and submissive in the extreme.[18] The desire for delicacy was so powerful that simulated illness became stylish. Such unconscious expressions of solidarity with women who contracted the disease may have served to somewhat anesthetize its dreaded impact.[19] But as the epidemic continued and hundreds of thousands of women died, an *embodied reaction* set in, and thin bodies became unfashionable. By 1880, popular medical theorists were equating amplitude and health. The large, hearty, buxom female body had become the model of beauty and (heterosexual) desirability, and it was no longer stylish to express solidarity with those who were ill.[20] Although the devastating impact of epidemic tuberculosis did not abate until well into the twentieth century (with the discovery of antibiotics), a voluptuous woman now symbolized, with her flesh, a specific form of denial.[21]

We see parallel forms of denial of AIDS operating in the generously fleshed bear body in which amplitude and health once again cohere. The bear—at least iconographically—embodies comfort, security, and safety, perhaps even evoking the polymorphous perversity of infancy. Susan Bordo's *Unbearable Weight: Feminism, Western Culture, and the Body* begins with a reading of Delmore Schwartz's poem "The Heavy Bear."[22] She suggests as part of an extended discussion that "the bear is above all else a creature of instinct, of primitive need. Ruled by orality, by hunger, blindly 'mouthing' experience, seeking honey and sugar, he is 'in love' . . . but with the most basic, infantile desires: to be soothed by sweet things, to discharge his hunger, to fall exhausted into stupor."[23]

We begin to see the bear publications as a set of what Kate calls "symptomatic texts" from which we can draw out discourses of gay male masculinity, but we are concerned about what conclusions we might reach. We wonder about the question of legitimacy—what grants us the right to say anything authoritative about constructions of gay male masculinity or sexual desire? Perhaps it is possible to look at bears as both challenge and inspiration. We wonder whether we are confronting a new gay male aesthetic in the process of defining itself both with and against the memories/experiences of other gay male aesthetics (for example, "queens," "clones," "swish") by both rejecting and incorporating elements of former styles?

We realize that further investigations are in order. Beth wants more texts; Kate suggests arranging a field trip to "Bear Night" at a local bar, with her bear friend as a guide. We decamp to the local gay bookstore where we behave entirely in character. Kate makes for the gay male porn rack and spends half an hour selecting a pile of possible titles. Beth, meanwhile, wanders through the lesbian theory and mystery sections, trying not to feel embarrassed. We ultimately converge on a sofa in the bookstore's bay window, sorting through the pile of magazines, picking a representative selection. When it comes time to pay, Beth hangs back: "You go ahead and pay, Kate—I just want to check something I was looking at earlier." Her hope is that Kate will explain the unusual nature of our purchases to the young woman at the register. Kate tries to brazen out the moment but nonetheless finds herself explaining our research to the amused clerk. On the way out of the store, we laugh ruefully. The Catholic confessional imperatives of childhood retain a powerful hold on both our adult imaginations despite the vast contextual dissonance between the white organdy dresses and veils of our First Holy Communions and this field trip to the porn rack at the queer bookstore.[24]

That evening, in her journal, Beth writes:

> Reading Ruth Behar tonight, I am struck by a realization.[25] Kate, with her insistence on attending to the bears' taxonomy that A. supplied from the Internet and on going with C. to the bear bar next week, is pushing me toward ethnography (with all its limitations). I, of course, am pulling her toward the textual analysis of the political theorist (with all its limitations). Thus we seem to become, at least methodologically, more partial, more tentative, perhaps more fluid with regard to our work as this process unfolds.

Both of us deal in theory, but from different disciplinary perspectives; Kate's field is critical film and media studies, subsumed by cultural theory, and Beth's is political theory, with a strong feminist bent. Despite the "failures" of socialist experiments over the past decade, we refuse to relinquish our shared belief in a utopian ideal of a society that would benefit everyone, satisfying human needs and nurturing human creativity despite differences of sex, sexual preference, gender, gender preference, color, culture, age, size, abilities, or class. Our tentativeness about our "right" to undertake this project is thus fueled by the same values that propel its urgency. On one hand, how can we not engage in questions of how identity is signaled by and through the human body, of the role of the physical in acquiring and maintaining gender and sexual identity, and of how human bodies become vehicles for self-presentation when all these are central to the political ideals of empowerment, dignity, and respect we want to encourage? On the other hand, when the identities in question are not—indeed can never be (or become)—our own, how could we?

We realize that we are holding here a number of tenuous strands of history, politics, and culture. Our awareness of and reluctance to play into any presumption that we as women, as a couple of fat dykes, can define experiences that are not and can never be our own is too much with us. Reluctantly, we conclude that ethnography is simply beyond us:

Kate: I realized I couldn't face the field trip to the bar—it just sounds too much like a roomful of men.

Beth: Well, wouldn't that be inevitable?

Kate: Yes, but I'd underestimated that aspect of it—

Beth: So pictures are one thing, the flesh quite another?

What we can do in these pages is raise some questions about possible readings and meanings of what we see in these snapshots (literal and metaphorical) of bears and bear culture, with an eye to alliance, not surveillance, border crossing, or invasion.

Configuring Gay Masculinity/Desire: The Bare/Bear Body

It may be easier to be gay or lesbian today than it was twenty years ago, but in a society that remains predicated on compulsory heterosexuality, being gay, lesbian, or any of the other "alternatives" does not represent a free or easy choice. Historians have only recently begun to map the configurations and constructions of queer lives and communities.[26] The real stories of what the earthshaking shifts in these configurations and constructions in the latter half of the twentieth century have meant to gay men remain largely untold. From McCarthyism and Mattachine to Stonewall, Gay Liberation, disco, and "Don't Ask, Don't Tell" and with the decimating force of the AIDS pandemic looming for more than fifteen years, homophobic myths promulgated by mainstream media (and at times by the gay media as well) have all too often gone uncontested, along with the tendencies toward erotophobia that have blossomed in straight and gay culture since 1980.

As lesbians aware of the complicated and intertwining strands of individuality, community, culture, sexuality, iconography, and other representational practices that go into the construction of any forms of desire, we can only begin to imagine the difficulties faced by gay men who have had to "grapple with an ever-changing terrain" in the "struggle to erect edifices of hope" in the wake of AIDS.[27] Even though this chapter is not about AIDS, it seems impossible to talk about historical configurations of gay masculinity or sexuality without some acknowledgment of AIDS's differential impact on our communities.[28]

The politics of sexuality is not "just" about community or lifestyle choices, however. It is about desire and the delicate balances of pleasure, danger, and power attached to or flowing from moments of sexual intimacy and/or vulnerability. But we know so little about these things. Speaking of lesbian constructions of "butch/femme" desire, Amber Hollibaugh acutely captures this problem:

> I don't think we know very much about what the erotic engine is that makes us move. . . . The ways that we've constructed our ideas of sexuality are very tiny. It's critical that we be able to say to each other that this is not about style, not about roles as though we put them on because we bought them in a store. It's about loving each other. It's about caring passionately about each other's existence. It's about feeling each other's mouths on each other's bodies. That isn't small. . . . The desire between us is the engine that moves us.[29]

In short, a politics of sexuality is about embodied sex, embodied desire, embodied commitment, and the categories we use to express them. We do not see any good reasons for distinguishing between lesbian and gay male sexualities at this juncture, at which desire and categories such as butch/femme or bear remain abstractions, although we acknowledge that in actual practice, theoretical similarities may not emerge clearly or at all. This does not diminish the conceptual or practical utility of categorical formulations of sexual desire in the least. As Gayle Rubin pointed out,

> Our categories are important. We cannot organize a social life, a political movement, or our individual identities and desires without them. The fact that categories invariably leak and can never contain all the relevant "existing things" does not render them useless, only limited. Categories like "woman," "butch," "lesbian," or "transsexual" are all imperfect, historical, temporary, and arbitrary. We use them, and they use us. We use them to construct meaningful lives, and they mold us into historically specific forms of personhood. Instead of fighting for immaculate classifications and impenetrable boundaries, let us strive to maintain a community that understands diversity as a gift, sees anomalies as precious, and treats all basic principles with a hefty dose of skepticism.[30]

The question becomes one of articulating the engines of desire that move bears forward (sexually and/or culturally), of distinguishing some of the categories in which these engines operate.

In an article by Les K. Wright entitled "The Sociology of The Urban Bear," we find a helpful set of insights into the representation of bears and their culture.[31] Although Wright admits to viewing bears "through the rose-colored glasses of an avid participant/observer" and his text is highly subjective, its main points are corroborated by other texts and testimonies. Wright asserts that "bears have been developing a new spiritual home, a social and sexual community that reflects a new simplicity and candor, a new matter-of-factness about erotic survival in a time when some of the most sexually repressive energy is emanating from the larger gay community."[32] We wonder at the emphasis on "new" in Wright's analysis—does he mean that before bears arrived on the scene, gay men lacked opportunities for building spiritual homes and creating community? We think it might be more productive to consider ways in which "newer"" and older cultural expressions might intersect and, in so doing, raise some interesting questions regarding gendered configurations and expressions of sexual desire.

The embodied representation of the bear, as we have already noted, is burly and hairy and/or full bearded, perhaps balding. This appears to be a conscious rejection of the Castro-clone style of gay masculinity dating from the 1970s. Wright criticizes the clone phenomenon as "a middle-class fetishization of working-class masculinity," which, while retaining an emphasis on status and slenderness, had attempted to stake out a middle ground between the extremely effeminate style of "queens" and the hypermasculinity of the "leather scene."[33] The bear sensibility is thus a rejection of a rejection, with multivalent trajectories. In other words, movement between and among multiple aspects of identity and other forms of "border crossing" becomes the order of the day. Bears thus must be conceived as engaged in the ongoing sociopolitical struggle in which many—gay men, lesbians, straight people—have been fighting to reclaim the erotic in the face of claims that "Sex = Death," injunctions to "Just Say No," and the similar expressions of erotophobia that have emerged alongside AIDS.

Even though the bear aesthetic may reject the macho ethic of the clone and may represent a significant departure from other configurations of gay male masculinity, it does not necessarily negate what has gone before. Indeed, it may equally well incorporate earlier cultural forms and styles in "both/and" constructions that militate against whole-cloth rejections predicated on the "either/or." Thus one might be simultaneously both swishy and bear or camp it up one minute and be a wild man the next, without erasing either experience. Ultimately, as Wright puts it, this means a "kind of reintegration [that might] make for spiritually sounder and emotionally healthier people—a bit more *Roseanne* (John Goodman makes a perfect bear), a bit less *Brideshead Revisited.*"[34]

An interesting variation on one of the major themes in recent feminist theory, the "ethic of care" articulated by Carol Gilligan, Virginia Held, Joan Tronto, and others, is incorporated by bear semiotics.[35] According to Wright, dissatisfaction with the "colored-hanky" semiotics by which a number of gay men had been signaling interest in specific sexual acts led some to replace hankies with small teddy bears in their back pockets, de-emphasizing the competitive, performance-based aspects of sex as sport: "Sticking a little teddy bear in your back pocket or shirt pocket was a way of saying 'I'm a human being. I give and receive affection.' "[36] The forging of common emotional bonds came to be represented in "a kind of protective tenderness" toward other men that is based on tolerance that crosses boundaries of class and race and is "attested by the social interaction between bears, the leather community . . . chubby chasers and daddy admirers" as well as those who are "recovering" or "clean and sober." The claim is that "an intense blend of purely physical lust and genuine affection and deeply experienced sense of community informs the bear movement," despite there being "as many scenes as there are people."[37]

Caretaking, tolerance, and affection have not been central to the orthodox masculinity of compulsory heterosexuality, nor do they appear to have figured strongly in the clone cultural expressions that emerged in gay male communities during the 1970s. If anything, the clone ethic appears to have been predicated on a nearly total rejection of all "feminine" behavioral forms, especially those associated with the effeminate stereotypes such as queens, sissies, and swishes. Nurturance was not salient to that discourse (although we suspect that it may have been more evident in practice than it was in rhetoric). It seems far more marked, however, in the rhetorical and iconographic public presentations of bears—clearly in fantasy and perhaps in actual practice.

In fictional accounts, the bear ethic of nurturance is literally embodied. The bear's body is permeable, his boundaries fluid enough to permit the exchange of both semen and affection, further signifying a generous incorporation of marginality in various forms. In "Lost Dad," the narrator befriends an older homeless man, and the two become lovers:

> "Oh Shawn," I found myself saying. "Be my daddy. Hold me in your arms. I want to be a little boy for just a little while.". . . Suddenly Shawn was getting up and sitting on the edge of the tub. In slow motion, the water ran off his large, hairy body. I watched, fascinated, as his fat, uncut cock came into view. Beneath it were two massive balls. The water ran off them in a single stream. I wanted to drink that water.[38]

Later, the narrator notices that he has come to orgasm without touching himself, one of the few times he has ever climaxed in that manner. The moment when he realizes this concretizes the bear's capacity for identification with, and nurturance of, the

Other: "Soon Shawn was asleep and snoring softly. As I lay there, content, I had a feeling the Shawn had found a home. I didn't know how long he would stay but I hoped it would be for a long time."[39]

The bear's "naturalness" may be expressed through an interest in body secretions. Witness a representative passage from "The Bruin" in which a young employee has sex with his boss:

> Holding onto his belt loops, I lowered my head and took that German sausage into my eager mouth, savoring the taste of his man-sweat, inhaling the ripe, musky aroma surrounding it. I pulled back the thick foreskin, revealing his mild, cheesy surprise, and lovingly licked and cleaned every speck with my tongue. . . . I swallowed every inch of his seasoned manhood.[40]

The earthy sensuality of the narrator is further evidenced in his description of the boss's bodily aroma: "a combination of sweat and inexpensive Daddy aftershave."[41]

Kate: I'm wondering whether this discourse of nurturance has to be presented through a discourse of sex in order to make it OK for men to participate? Or is it a way of reclaiming the whole body for eroticism and thereby de-phallicizing the cock? And besides the nurturance, what about the playfulness? I think that really mitigates my discomfort with the wild man myth's seeming to reproduce old time sexism.

Beth: You know, I can't help going back to the guy in the hammock with his cock sticking out. When I got past thinking "that looks painful," it became funny. It's really funny. And yes, it's very playful.

Unraveling the skeins of one's own desire is no easy task, let alone approaching other tangled weaves. We see in the bear texts a valorization of the ur-butch "wild man" who may not be very far removed from Sam Keen's vision of the "fierce gentleman."[42] The wild-man aspect of the gay bear evokes a natural creature, untamed by culture and unfettered by prudish convention. He is "at home" in his body as it is, comfortable with its girth, growths, and secretions, unafraid to encounter his primal self. The wild bear is free in a way that no one else is—not only to satisfy his hunger[43] but also to venture into the dark cave of his own "feminine" unconscious. His life cycle represents a symbiosis of conscious/unconscious, rational/emotional. He may appear at one moment as the fierce grizzly, at the next the playful, cuddly teddy (who is also a play*mate*)—and back again. Power, pleasure, and danger hang in his balance.

What or, indeed, whom does the "wild man" represent? The claim is that bear images "play on romanticized fantasies which blend sexual 'freedom' with 'frontier living' with 'independence,' and blur distinctions between frontiersmen—the simple, unfettered lives of trappers, loggers, hunters—and the wild-animal-man object of their desire."[44] Can this be taken at face value? Or is there perhaps something radically subversive of orthodox masculinity at work here, despite all the butch trappings? Might not bears represent the sort of "marginalized men" that Susan Bordo describes as "bearers of the shadow of the phallus, who have been the alchemical agents disturbing the (deceptively) stable elements" of orthodox masculinity in a newly percolating social psyche?[45]

What spaces are available for gay self-representation(s) and the forging of collective identities in the mid-1990s? Are the images and rhetoric of bears more consonant with the process of bricolage, in which available signs and practices are manipulated and revalued within historically specific cultural parameters, than with a whole-cloth adoption of tropes of orthodox masculinity?[46] How and why are these particular "signs and practices" chosen and embodied? Is there something here about refusals—"just saying no" to being bound by certain standards that regulate and sanitize the body? If you are part of a culture in which many people have spent or are spending considerable time in hospitals—you might not be sick, but your friends and lovers are—or if you're frustrated trying to make sense of the often contradictory, sometimes useless, but always clinical rhetoric surrounding "safe sex," wouldn't you want to resist the medicalization of the body? Is there a logic to the appeal of sweaty, smelly, organic, raunchy, wet stuff that makes sex "dirty" again—as it ought to be? And what about the power of desire—in all its seductive, and perhaps profoundly patriarchal, glory?

In bear culture, the locus of desire appears to be fairly consistently articulated in terms of sameness and by the desiring subject. One of the more interesting ways in which this plays out is with the valorization of age in the daddy figure, which may incorporate intergenerational relations between older (or dominant) daddy bears and younger (or submissive) cubs. Daddy-boy roles appear in leather and other gay male subcultures, but in the bear subculture, a specific, differentiated meaning is attached. Daddy bears are mature in the sense that they know themselves and their own desires. They are strong, manly, and at the same time unashamed to express their feelings of affection and need. Daddy bears are generous, indulgent, and tactile. As with all things sexual, multivalent meanings and symbols abound. Is a desire for daddy an expression of longing for protection and nurturance or of wishing to draw close to phallic power or some combination of both or something else entirely?

We think it is important to differentiate between the meanings of father and daddy here. Father is often absent, all but aural: the god in the sky whose name cannot be inscribed. He is the ultimate locus of the unknowable, of phallocentric power and authority—a strong, silent type. "Father Bear" in the Goldilocks story gets the big chair, the big bowl, the hard bed (the hard-on?). He clearly wears the phallus in his household. In modern Western societies, the father also signifies the ultimate enforcement of sanctions against effeminate behavior by boys.[47] Alienation and estrangement are what make Father most himself. When Father is most himself, he is "not-Mother." Her boundaries are always already permeable and often entirely dissolved—which may be the real source of both her power and his envy.

Daddy, on the other hand, is a metaphor of companionship, not conquest or competition. Children play with "Daddy." There are the games of catch in the backyard, the pillow fights at bedtime. You can get dirty with Daddy. His love is warm, all-enfolding, unconditional—at a far remove from the severe father who doles out punishment, apparently arbitrarily, yet always for your own good.

Is "Daddy" perhaps always already inscribed as fantasy in

some gay male imaginations? Age itself, with all its connotations—girth, wrinkles, gray hair, hair loss—may offer magical properties to the "daddy" phenomenon among bears and other gay male subcultures in which the role appears. For many gay men, the very idea of getting old, or at least living past forty, has taken on new meaning. We both recall conversations with lesbian and gay male friends around 1980, a time when we all were turning or approaching thirty. Many dykes embraced this. As Beth put it, "Thirty meant you could start not giving a shit as a woman and getting away with it." But for many gay men, it meant you were over the hill, you were never going to get a date. The memory of these discussions is grim because so many of the men who feared thirty never made it to forty.

If daddy is a magical figure, the stuff of fantasy or reality, what does it mean to fuck him? Or be fucked by him? Is there perhaps a call here to retheorize the oedipal trajectory in which the father is introjected in the total absence of the mother? What role might the mother play *in absentia?* Do the connections to "ethics of care" articulated earlier demand that we search, at least interpretively, for a maternal subtext that might, as Coppélia Kahn puts it, demonstrate "the imprint of mothering on the male psyche, the psychological presence of the mother in men whether or not mothers are represented in the texts they write"?[48] In other words, do all three bears in the fairy tale become one here, mutually introjecting and resisting simultaneously in a perfect postmodernist moment that radically re-visions and re-writes a narrative of relational (de-phallocentric) authority?

Here we return to the question of categories of desire and the ways in which they may be deployed strategically, subversively, and politically. Although some aspects of reconfigured sexuality, desire, embodiment, and gay masculinity emerge clearly from the bear texts and discourse, others, especially those attached to race and class, are more complicated. Both class and race are discursively addressed in the bear texts, to a degree that is not evident in heterosexual pornography or other commodified forms of heterosexuality. The cultural meanings of this discourse, however, are unclear. Why, we wonder, do bears feel the need to adopt a rhetoric of racial inclusivity when the iconography of the texts before us is so overwhelmingly white? Why is so much emphasis placed on significations of working-class identity? To what political ends are these stylistic forms deployed?

The rhetorical assertion forwarded by bear proponents of inclusivity is simple. Wright, for example, suggests that as opposed to the "middle-class fetishization of working class masculinity" noted earlier as a central component of clone culture, the "subcultures of leathersex, bears, and the vast working-class gay population of San Francisco intersect in the assertion of an openly and genuinely working-class homosexual ethic."[49] Although not all bears belong to the working class, the claim is that their "sociosexual adhesiveness has its roots in a Whitmanesque democratic appreciation of the common man" in which "working-class white gay men are discovering that they have more, sometimes much more, in common with one another and with working-class black or Latino gay men than they do with middle-class gay men of any color."[50] Indeed, bear gatherings may strive for a particular ambience of openness, at which "men of all shapes and sizes and ages and races and sexual interests converge "with "little or none of the old bath-house tension." A "model type," for example, is described as having "left a recent bear party within 20 minutes, once he realized his buffed appearance didn't draw instant adulation."[51]

Some aspects of the bear discourses of sexuality and gender that we examined do seem to configure a new democratization of gay male sexual relations in the wake of AIDS. The texts emphasize participant observation to a high degree and utilize tropes largely absent from earlier configurations of gay male sexual desire: associations to gritty, working-class experiences (truckers, gimme caps, auto mechanics, flannel shirts, mountain men, etc.) juxtaposed with naked, hairy bodies that would not be deemed "model" in any other context. The images themselves, along with accompanying texts of formula fiction, promote a general sensuality that remains rough, natural, and organic while simultaneously incorporating humor. As Kate observed, these are spaces where "men can look like they're aging, and still have their tits played with."

The publications we studied, even those clearly produced for a mass market, retain a grassroots sensibility more evocative of locally produced, photocopied "zines" than of the slick, glossy pages we have come to associate with gay male porn.[52] But how democratized are the cultural spaces they depict? For one thing, the images presented are, almost without exception, white and only rarely identifiable as "ethnic" in any way. Despite the textual claims that in bear culture, racial and socioeconomic boundaries are routinely crossed, we are skeptical: African American men, or men of any color (besides white), are depicted or described only in the personals—and here, as in the editorial copy, whiteness predominates. A few ads describe men with disabilities, but no images of physically challenged individuals appeared in the publications we examined.

Although a full exploration of how the complicated relations of race and class shape constructions of gay or straight masculinity is beyond the scope of this chapter, we want to put some cautionary brakes on any facile claims regarding the democratization of bear cultural spaces and productions. The bear public sphere may present an opening for democracy in a particular gay male cultural space, but there is little evidence in the texts we examined to show that bears have made significant strides away from privileging whiteness and/or middle-class masculinity. A rhetoric valorizing inclusivity and working-class experience is certainly present, but we see no movement toward questioning the contradictions between rhetoric and reality in the pages of these texts. Why aren't letters to the editors questioning the whiteness of the images? What is really going on if CPAs don blue jeans and doff gimme caps when they go off to a party weekend on Friday afternoon only to return to a corporate uniform of suits and ties (and collect higher paychecks) come Monday? Given the intensification of class polarization over the past decade, what does it mean when lawyers masquerade as automobile mechanics or assembly-line workers? Where in these texts are the voices of "Other" bears—men marked not by whiteness but by color, ethnicity, disability, and the like?

There may be openings among the bears for new possibilities, new cultural, social, and political configurations of gay male desire, new constructions of gender—and thereby new possibilities for solidarity, alliance, and community among lesbians and gay men. However, we recognize that any conclusive determinations in this regard will have to come out of analyses undertaken by those who are able to participate in, as well as observe, the bear cultural universe. For when all is said and done, we remain, with Goldilocks, uninvited guests among the bears.

Notes

1. "A man is like a bear: the uglier, the prettier." Beth's friend Michael Forman recalled this favorite saying of his mother from his childhood in Bogotá, Colombia. When asked to provide its provenance, however, she could not remember when she learned the aphorism or in what context. We thank Forman for sharing this and for providing helpful commentary on early versions of this essay, as did Kevin Cathcart, Frida Furman, Sandra Jackson, Ann Russo, and Jackie Taylor. Thanks are also due to Gene Sampson for his superb clerical support and generous good humor and to Craig Kois for his insights and friendship.

2. Then there's the ick factor. See chapter 4 in this volume.

3. Elizabeth A. Kelly, "Grounds for Criticism: Coffee, Passion, and the Politics of Feminist Discourse," in Lois Lovelace Duke, ed., *Women in Politics: Outsiders or Insiders?* rev. ed. (Upper Saddle River, N.J.: Prentice-Hall, 1996), pp. 351–368; see also Elizabeth A. Kelly, *Education, Democracy, and Public Knowledge* (Boulder, Colo.: Westview Press, 1995).

4. See bell hooks, "Eating the Other: Desire and Resistance," in bell hooks, *Black Looks: Race and Representation* (Boston: South End Press, 1992), pp. 21–39. For hooks, "eating the Other" describes "the Eurocentric habit of consuming images of exotics (those marked by color, ethnicity, and/or other forms of difference)." In the case of gay men,

however, definitions of the desiring subject/desired object, either or both may be Other; thus an Asian man who likes Asian men can call himself a rice queen.

5. As in the 1960s Hanna-Barbera cartoon series, Yogi Bear. Boo-Boo was Yogi's sidekick.

6. At a number of points we recalled the early Michigan Women's Music Festivals, with dykes going bananas because here, finally, was a safe space where we could take off our T-shirts and get sunburned "down to there."

7. *BEAR* 38, p. 21.

8. *Classic BEAR* 13.

9. See Nancy Fraser, "Rethinking the Public Sphere: A Contribution to the Critique of Actually Existing Democracy," *Social Text* 25/26 (Winter 1990): 56–80, for a provocative treatment of the concept of alternative public spheres.

10. Rangercub, "From a Cub's-Eye View," *Heavy Duty Premier,* July–September 1996, pp. 33–35.

11. David Tilton, "Intercourse with Steve Blanscet, Mr. International Bear 1996," *American Bear* 3, p. 13.

12. Jürgen Habermas, *The Structural Transformation of the Public Sphere: An Inquiry into a Category of Bourgeois Society,* trans. Thomas Burger with the assistance of Frederick Lawrence (Cambridge, Mass.: MIT Press, 1989); see also Craig Calhoun, ed., *Habermas and the Public Sphere* (Cambridge, Mass.: MIT Press, 1985); and David Rasmussen, ed., *Universalism vs. Communitarianism: Contemporary Debates in Ethics* (Cambridge, Mass.: MIT Press, 1990). For a specifically feminist analysis, see Joan B. Landes, *Women and the Public Sphere in the Age of the French Revolution* (Ithaca, N.Y.: Cornell University Press, 1988).

13. She suspects that this habit was formed while she was in utero, when her lonely, pregnant mother read aloud from women's magazines in order to hear the sound of a human voice—even if it was her own.

14. *ClassicBEAR,* pp. 15–16; *BEAR,* pp. 38, 68.

15. As a number of lesbian theorists have argued, we are perhaps more powerfully charged with the erotic than women have traditionally

been socialized to admit—or this sort of language reflects. See, for example, Audre Lorde's classic "Uses of the Erotic: The Erotic as Power," in Audre Lorde, *Sister Outsider: Essays and Speeches* (Trumansburg, N.Y.: Crossing Press, 1984), pp. 53–59.

16. See Yvonne Tasker, *Spectacular Bodies: Gender, Genre, and the Action Cinema* (London: Routledge, 1993), for a discussion of the hard body and penetrability.

17. Barbara Ehrenreich and Deirdre English, *For Her Own Good: 150 Years of the Experts' Advice to Women* (Garden City, N.Y.: Doubleday/ Anchor, 1979).

18. Lois Banner, *American Beauty* (Chicago: University of Chicago Press, 1983), pp. 51–52.

19. Mary Wollstonecraft, for instance, scathingly criticized women "who have fostered a romantic, unnatural delicacy" for their "docility and . . . spaniel-like affection." Mary Wollstonecraft, *A Vindication of the Rights of Woman* (1792; reprint, Buffalo, N.Y.: Prometheus Books, 1989), pp. 41, 43.

20. Banner, *American Beauty,* p. 51.

21. Ibid., pp. 106–107.

22. Delmore Schwartz, "The Heavy Bear," from Delmore Schwartz, *Selected Poems: Summer Knowledge* (New York: New Directions, 1959), quoted in Susan Bordo, *Unbearable Weight: Feminism, Western Culture, and the Body* (Berkeley and Los Angeles: University of California Press, 1993); for Bordo's reading of the poem, see pp. 2–15.

23. Bordo, *Unbearable Weight,* p. 2.

24. For a discussion of recent "lesbian style wars" and the construction of lesbian aesthetics, see Arlene Stein, "All Dressed up but No Place to Go? Style Wars and the New Lesbianism," in Corey K. Creekmur and Alexander Doty, eds., *Out in Culture: Gay, Lesbian, and Queer Essays on Popular Culture* (Durham, N.C.: Duke University Press, 1995), pp. 476–483.

25. The texts explored in this essay are *AMERICAN BEAR* no. 13, June/July 1996; *BEAR* 38, June 1996; *CR (Chiron Rising Magazine),* 74, June–July 1996; *ClassicBEAR,* February 1996; *DADDY: The Magazine* 28,

June 1996; *Daddybear* 3 (n.d.); and *Heavy Duty Premier,* July–September 1996.

26. Behar writes, "With all the discussion of ethnographic writing going on at the moment, so little is said about how each of us comes to the pen and the computer and the authority to speak and author texts ... authorship is a privilege to which many of us are not born, but arrive at, often clumsily, often painfully, often through a process of self-betrayal and denial ... authorship is a privilege constituted by the gender, sociohistorical background, and class origins, or lately class diasporas, of the anthropologist doing the writing." We suggest that this applies equally well to other "social scientists," indeed to any of us who write about cross-cultural encounters. Ruth Behar, *Translated Woman: Crossing the Border with Esperanza's Story* (Boston: Beacon Press, 1993), p. 338.

27. See, for example, Allan Bérubé, *Coming out under Fire* (New York: Free Press, 1990); George Chauncey, *Gay New York: Gender, Urban Culture, and the Making of the Gay Male World 1890–1940* (New York: Basic Books, 1994); John D'Emilio, *Sexual Politics, Sexual Communities: The Making of a Homosexual Minority in the United States, 1940–1970* (Chicago: University of Chicago Press, 1983); Martin Bauml Duberman, Martha Vicinus, and George Chauncey Jr., eds., *Hidden from History: Reclaiming the Gay and Lesbian Past* (New York: New American Library, 1989); Lillian Faderman, *Odd Girls and Twilight Lovers: A History of Lesbian Life in Twentieth Century America* (New York: Columbia University Press, 1991); Elizabeth Lapovsky Kennedy and Madeline D. Davis, *Boots of Leather, Slippers of Gold: The History of a Lesbian Community* (New York: Penguin Books, 1994).

28. Eric Rofes, *Reviving the Tribe: Regenerating Gay Men's Sexuality and Culture in the Ongoing Epidemic* (New York: Harrington Park Press, 1996). Rofes's courageous documentation of how this task has been complicated by the sheer rapidity of changes in gay masculinity, the institutional possibilities of gay sexual experience, and the configuration of gay desire over the past three or four decades is provocative and insightful.

29. For provocative thinking on this, see Judith McDaniel and Judith Mazza, "Safe Sex for Lesbians: What's It All About?" and Amber Hollibaugh, "Transmission, Transmission, Where's the Transmission?" both in Karen Kahn, ed., *Front Line Feminism, 1975–1995: Essays from Sojourner's First 20 Years* (San Francisco: Aunt Lute Books, 1995), pp. 277–280, 281–287; also Katie J. Hogan, " 'Victim Feminism' and the Complexities of AIDS" in Nan Bauer Maglin and Donna Perry, eds., *Bad Girls: Women, Sex, and Power in the Nineties* (New Brunswick, N.J.: Rutgers University Press, 1996), pp. 68–89.

30. "A celebration of butch–femme identities in the lesbian community," a panel discussion held at the New York Lesbian and Gay Community Service Center, December 6, 1990. The panelists included Sue Hyde, Amber Hollibaugh, Deanna Alida, Lisa Winters, Val Tavai, Jewelle Gomez, Jill Harris, and Joan Nestle, with Stephanie Grant moderating; in Joan Nestle, ed. *The Persistent Desire: A Femme–Butch Reader* (Boston: Alyson Publications, 1992), pp. 454–463.

31. Gayle Rubin, "Of Catamites and Kings: Reflections on Butch, Gender, and Boundaries," in Joan Nestle, ed. *The Persistent Desire: A Femme–Butch Reader* (Boston: Alyson Publications, 1992), pp. 466–482, 477.

32. Les K. Wright, "The Sociology of the Urban Bear," *Drummer* 140, June 1990, reprinted in *ClassicBEAR* (1996): 53–55.

33. Ibid., p. 53.

34. Ibid.

35. Ibid.

36. Carol Gilligan, *In A Different Voice: Psychological Theory and Women's Development* (Cambridge, Mass.: Harvard University Press, 1982); Virginia Held, *Feminist Morality: Transforming Culture, Society, and Politics* (Chicago, University of Chicago Press, 1993); and Joan Tronto, *Moral Boundaries: A Political Argument for an Ethic of Care* (New York: Routledge, 1993). Uma Narayan's cogent reminder that "while contemporary care discourse correctly insists on acknowledging human needs and relationships, it needs to worry about who defines these often contested terms" is worth noting here. Uma Narayan, "Colo-

nialism and Its Others: Considerations on Rights and Care Discourses," *Hypatia* 10 (Spring 1995): 133–140; 133.

37. Wright, "Sociology of the Urban Bear," p. 54.

38. Ibid.

39. Nicholas Mann, "Lost Dad," *DaddyBear* 3, p. 18.

40. Ibid., p. 19. Once again, note the similarity in tone to formula romance in women's magazines.

41. Boomer, "The Bruin," *DaddyBear* 3, p. 33.

42. Ibid.

43. Sam Keen, *Fire in the Belly: On Being a Man* (New York: Bantam, 1992), p. 112.

44. See the Delmore Schwartz poem cited earlier.

45. Wright, "Sociology of the Urban Bear," p. 53.

46. Bordo, "Reading the Male Body," p. 281.

47. Christine di Stefano notes that such sanctions are "consistent . . . with the suggestion that modern masculinity resembles a reaction formation rather than an originary model of selfhood. As such, it is unstable and vulnerable, particularly to the 'polluting' influence of feminine elements. A rigid enforcement of masculine norms of behavior suggests a powerful horror at the prospect of mixing or confusing cherished and vulnerable categories." See Christine DiStefano, *Configurations of Masculinity: A Feminist Perspective on Modern Political Theory* (Ithaca, N.Y.: Cornell University Press, 1991), p. 46.

48. Coppélia Kahn, "Excavating 'Those Dim Minoan Regions': Maternal Subtexts in Patriarchal Literature," *Diacritics: A Review of Contemporary Criticism* 12 (Summer 1982): 36.

49. *ClassicBEAR*, p. 53.

50. Ibid., p. 54.

51. Ibid., p. 55.

52. See Richard Dyer, "Don't Look Now: The Instabilities of the Male Pinup," in Richard Dyer, *Only Entertainment* (New York: Routledge, 1992), pp. 121–134.

C H A  P T E R

The Butch/Femme Dance: Two-Stepping along the Gender Line

Lawrence Schimel

When I think of sexiness in a woman, I think of glamour. Rita Hayworth as Gilda. Luxuriant hair, the gentle curve of hip and breast. Soft, thick lips. A total femme. The kind of woman I imagine myself to be, to have that power to attract men.

In real life, that's not the kind of woman I'm attracted to.

The fact that I'm attracted to women at all is somewhat disturbing to my identity as a gay man. But it happens all the time. There's a certain kind of butch dyke who looks like a cute college-aged boy. I'll cruise her on the streets of Chelsea without realizing it. In a mixed club or event, these girls are almost always cuter than the biological boys. They're giving me all the cues I'm wired, as a gay man, to respond to and I do: I respond, and I feel cheated and embarrassed when I realize my mistake. I'm not interested in these women once I realize they are women. I want them as the men they portray, that persona of masculinity that seems to click so often with my visual "type."

It's not that I'm just getting nearsighted and am cruising anything in pants that walks with a wide stance. These women seem to fall so effortlessly into certain masculine characteristics—better than most men do. And perhaps that's the trick. They've had to pay more attention, to watch how we construct "male" and "female," and they're now choosing what they want to use to represent themselves. Women have had to learn how to portray that femme glamour that is artifice and construct, no matter how effortless and natural it seems, no matter how many times society tells us it's "intrinsic" to womanhood.

Butch women choose to ignore that cultural knowledge, to exclude it from themselves. Maybe that's what turns me on. I know that a mix is what I find sexy, the dynamic of that attraction overlaid on bodies that are the same. I've never understood how gay men seem oblivious to butch/femme dynamics between men and why it is not part of our culture, certainly not part of our commercialized sexual media and pornography. When I edited *Switch Hitters: Lesbians Write Gay Male Erotica and Gay Men Write Lesbian Erotica* with Carol Queen, I hoped that some of the lesbian contributors would address butch/femme dynamics between men, thereby introducing these ideas into the marketplace of gay pornography. But they did not; the women repeated and sustained the tropes and stereotypes of gay pornography, adhering to the formulas.

Gay pornography mimics the homophobia of a heterosexual locker room: effeminacy is taboo in this land of machismo and bravado as one big beefy guy boringly boffs another big beefy guy on screen. Gay men too often adopt these prepackaged images wholesale, claiming them as their desire, without ever wondering what their desires really are. The very idea of a femme man violates some nebulous and unrealized social construct of masculinity. We've adopted the heterosexual mindframe of femme men as undesirable, emasculated, antimen. The gay personal ads reading "no fats, femmes, or druggies" are as innumerable as the grains of sand on the shores of South Beach or P-Town. We call femme men "nelly" and "sissies" and "faggots," taunts and slurs we've adopted from our straight tormentors. The male gender is blindly and simplistically used—by gays and straights alike—as shorthand for butch. There are no "male" words to describe the attraction to a man who does not fit this high-steroid profile.

I am a man and I am a femme. I still am young enough that my femme qualities are classically attractive to gay men as youthfulness. I am thin, lithe, smooth. A lover nicknamed me "Mowgli," the man-cub from Kipling's *Jungle Book,* and I exult in the comparison, the image, the body type. (Sabu!) The man who gave me this moniker was ten years my elder, not quite my daddy, but I was his boy, which is the closest gay men come to realizing the butch/femme dynamic that our female queer sisters understand better.

What will happen to my desirability, my sexuality, when I am an older man and still a femme? At some point I will cease to be a boy. Must I become a daddy then, by default? As an older gay man, must I be pigeonholed as a tired old queen or a troll, a dandy or a fop if I am not a daddy? Is there no room for an adult femme male (the kind of man I'll grow up to be) to be sexually desirable in this queer culture that so prioritizes the butch male (the kind of man I desire?)

I am a femme, and butch energy will always attract me, regardless of gender. Lately, women have begun to cruise me, too. And I'm not talking about the narrow-minded sort who want to "reclaim" me for heterosexuality, although there are those around on the fringes as well. I'm talking about butch dykes who want me as a gay man, about someone who doesn't want me to want her as a woman; she's interested in me only if she can be a man and take me as a man.

I haven't a clue what to do.

That is, I flirt back, of course. I'm a femme. We play the dance.

But what the hell should I really do?

One woman in particular has tempted me in part because she's been so persistent. Our professional lives overlap occasionally—conferences, book tours, social visits to our respective cities. I'd seen her give talks, readings from her work, I'd seen photographs of her—with flexed biceps, close-cropped black hair, a leather jacket, sometimes a cigar—when she won a medal as a body-builder. But the first time we actually met she was on a panel about sexuality at some ungodly hour of the morning, the second or third day of a conference, and I was groggily sitting in the audience wondering why I was awake so early. She said nice things about *Switch Hitters,* even though it had not yet been published. I was suddenly awake. The little part of my brain that speaks for my ego was jumping up and down in excitement: she knew who I was! And what's more, she liked me, liked my work.

I went up to her after the panel and introduced myself. As we talked, I got the definite feeling she liked me in a way I wasn't used to responding to, not from a woman. It confused me. At the same time, I found myself attracted to her butch energy. I found myself attracted to her courting and pursuit.

She asked me questions: intimate, male questions. What does an erection feel like? Can you ejaculate without orgasm? Can you have orgasm without ejaculation? A barrage of questions (and at that ungodly hour!).

I told her I'd answer her later, and I did, that night. In the interim, I'd hooked up with a nice kinky Jewish boy, a young thirtysomething daddy, ten years older than myself. We mirrored each other: ethnicity, upbringing, neuroses. He might have been me a decade from now. She, too, had found a partner for the evening, a soft-looking woman with close-cropped hair, about her age but Caucasian. Difference at play for her, narcissism for me.

We chatted, the four of us, two boys on one couch, two girls on the other. The boys held hands. The girls sometimes leaned against each other.

But we were flirting, she and I, and we both knew it.

Certainly I was flirting, too, with the boy I was with—flirting after the fact, since we'd each already decided to spend the night together and had been on our way to his room when she distracted me. We got a lot of nosy questions out of the way, he and I, before we went up to his room and had sex. We told each other what we liked, what we wanted, even though none of this was overtly for each other but directed at her, in answer to her questions.

In some ways I was reaffirming my identity as a gay boy to her—and to myself. I was proving my masculinity, in the locker-room bravado of sexual conquest. She merely smiled and waited.

When we next met, she continued to court me. Nothing had changed, except we now knew more about each other, about ourselves, about what we wanted.

She wanted to be my daddy, and I wanted to be her femme.

We talked more. We each went back to our rooms alone.

Our lives overlap occasionally—conferences, book tours, social visits to our respective cities. She continues to pursue me. I continue to enjoy being pursued.

What could equal this desiring?

We question each other and ourselves.

We flirt. We play the dance.

For now, that is enough.

CHAPTER 

Another Place to Breathe

Jewelle Gomez, Amber Hollibaugh, and Gayle Rubin

Jewelle Gomez, Amber Hollibaugh, and Gayle Rubin are lesbian activists and writers who have known one another over the last two decades as friends and colleagues. They met again with Sara Miles in San Francisco in early 1996 to talk about the impact of gay men's sex cultures on lesbian culture and of gay male sexuality on their own. This is an edited transcript of the afternoon's discussion.

Amber Hollibaugh: The mythology has been that boys are sexual and girls are not. It's gay men who are promiscuous and lesbians who are monogamous. Those have been the overarching constructs for a lot of community perception and community identification, whether they're true or not.

So to me, it also makes me think of why I felt close to gay male sexuality for a long time. It wasn't really about the practices so much as the sexual culture, the right to explicit sexual culture and to sexual identities—as different from homosexual identities. Your sexual orientation wasn't challenged by what your sexual practice was.

In the lesbian community, you had to be the right kind of lesbian, or you were suspected of not being a lesbian. And that was true in everything from butch/femme and S/M to a whole variety of identity-merger sexual practices. So gay male sexuality, for me, was kind of an umbrella, a protectionist umbrella for being gay, for being sexual the way that you needed to be, without having to give up your homosexuality.

Gayle Rubin: I think problems arise when people generalize about lesbian sexuality or lesbian sexual culture and gay male sexuality or gay male sexual culture. Both these need to be pluralized. What you're talking about, Amber, in terms of lesbian values regarding sex really has to do with a particular lesbian population that was very influenced by lesbian feminism as a political ideology and tended to organize lesbianism around that ideology. I think you are referring to the political lesbian culture and community and the ideologies of that population, which shouldn't be generalized to the entire lesbian population.

I actually think that if you take the whole population of lesbians and the whole population of gay men, what you will find are overlapping ranges of sexual ideologies that are present in both groups but distributed differently. And you'll probably find a lot of overlapping ideas as well as distinctive notions of sexual conduct and propriety.

One of the biggest differences is that at least in recent history, gay men have had a kind of institutionalized and commercial sexual culture that lesbians have lacked, and that's had a big impact on how both populations perceive themselves and are perceived by outsiders.

Jewelle Gomez: I think, for me, gay male sexuality has always had kind of a conflicting impact. Since it was the only visible homosexuality, even when it was invisible, it was implied. I think of reading James Baldwin and reading *Giovanni's Room* and having male sexuality be palpable on the pages and my identification with it as a lesbian because that was the only homosexual reference point I had. . . .

So in many ways, gay male sexuality historically represented a liberation simply because it was visible. On the other hand, I think for me, it's always evoked traditional male oppression because gay men exist in their sexuality in the privilege of having sex free of politics—in a way. Even though, of course, there is heterosexism, they're not suffering under a recognizable form of sexism throughout their growing up, through their adolescence and into adulthood, so that their practice of sex is privileged in a way that women have had to work through to get to in our practice of sex.

I feel that the period in which lesbian feminism developed its position on sexuality as oppressive, or male sexuality as oppressive, as exploitive, is an understandable part of a process of coming to sexual power. But women as people who have been the target of male sexuality in this society needed to grow through that, through what has come to be thought of as puritanical lesbian feminism, in order to find a way to that open expression of sexuality that men take for granted. And unfortunately, some women never found their way through and are still kind of stuck there.

I know when the big fight about closing the baths happened in New York . . . 1985 or 1986, something like that, I was one of three women on the board of the group that was starting GLAAD. The whole idea that there were baths, number one, that men had the economic freedom to create a place to have sex, was something I had to think about. I knew the baths were there. I knew that men owned all the discos and went to the discos, which were another place for sexual expression. So until it was raised as something that was about to be taken away, I simply thought of those as places of privilege. And then working with other women and men to militate against the closing of the baths, I started to see gay men start to realize that their privilege was not as widespread as they thought. Or as absolute.

And that, to me, was interesting because for the first time, I think, men started to see their sexual expression as vulnerable. With AIDS it really began, but with the closing of the baths and establishments like that, the idea that men could see themselves and their sexuality as being demonized and threatened, I think was significant politically.

I was in a community of lesbians for whom sexuality was always a danger. People still feel so oppressed, and it's because they still see male power as the most dominant power in this culture. And women still see ourselves as victims.

Gayle: I think we should talk about some of these ideas—for instance, that sexuality, if it's sort of easy, is male. That if it's easy, it's oppressive. That if it's male, it's oppressive. There are a number of words that get linked together very often, and I think we need to deconstruct them.

You brought up, Jewelle, one of the issues that is really central to these discussions, and that is the whole matter of historical reference points and context and how much those dominate one's sense of appropriate desire versus how detached they can be.

I think all desires are historically shaped, so it's not like they ever don't have context. However, in my experience of lesbian feminism and feminist ideas about sexuality, a particular notion of historical context becomes the privileged reference point. Evaluating things in those terms tends to make sexual desire subordinate to these political and moral considerations. This contrasts with an attitude more common in gay male culture, where people are not as concerned with context. There are men who care about that, but they seem fewer. I know a lot of guys who think, "If it gets my dick hard, it's fine. Why do I need to care about all this other stuff?"

They're not talking about "if it gets my dick hard, it's OK to rape someone." They're talking about "if I'm in a bathhouse or if I'm on a date with someone I like and something gets my dick hard, why should I care about what else it might have meant in some other context? It's not here. We're having fun, we're on a date, let's do it." A lot of the gay men I know just don't feel the need to evaluate every lust in terms of what historical connections it might have to some bad thing that they actually may, in fact, disapprove of. They're not as obsessed with purifying their desires of potentially evil associations. They don't seem to undergo the kind of self-examination or discussion or indecision around lust that a lot of women and lesbians tend to engage in.

Jewelle: That goes back to the position of victimization. I think women still feel victimized in this society around their sexuality, which is why women feel that they have to keep that history the dominant thing. Rape is still a threat shadowing every woman. And men feel less vulnerable, so they can make those separations and not consider history.

Gayle: Women have, in fact, had to pay, on the whole, much higher prices for being sexually active than men. So of course, being sexually active is imbued with a lot of fear. But you could argue that this is a product of oppression and that indulging it caters to some of the ways in which women have been systematically mistreated.

Amber: I'll argue that. I do argue that. That's part of why it's been so provocative, part of what I think that the fighting over sexual terrain and the kind of gendering of sexual terrain has been a such complicated dialogue.

Some of us were really trying to hold out for a sex-radical perspective in the context of our own histories as women, in lesbian and gay communities where we wanted pleasure to be something that we had a right to, without having to explain it to people all the time, where we had a right to take sexual chances and be a part of sexual danger. And that wasn't something that we expected feminism to remove from our sexual terrain.

That's still a very, very difficult conversation. For me, that's one of the things that's the most tragic about lesbian sexuality: I think for a lot of women, the price of trying to come out has been so high, on top of just the price of being female and sexual in our culture, that trying to integrate power and danger and marginality as an ongoing part of your sexuality is devastating.

Part of my read on lesbian feminism and its resulting narrowness around sexuality is that women are tired. Tired, tired, tired. It's like tired of hurting, tired of being scared, tired of everything. . . . And so the sexuality that ended up getting articulated from that was a sexuality of safety from sex and a really problematic relationship to pleasure and to being a sexual actor. And some of us, as tired as we might be, have never wanted to give that up. I mean, my own sexuality is fundamentally grounded in danger.

A lot of women I know felt their sexuality that way: always around power and always around danger. It's not like I never had a nice orgasm. But somehow in my mind, my imagination is fueled by danger. And I need it. I need it to feel things. Some of what I have always taken from gay male sexuality is the play and danger, the combination of those two things. I've also taken from a lot of other parts of gay male sexuality, long before this current period. Like drag, and bars, mixed bars, and the leather community. . . . I wanted their atmosphere of a kind of sexual—

Jewelle: Intensity.

Amber: Intensity. That all marginalized communities live within. And that was very important to me about gay male sexuality. They play, they try things out. They didn't decide that something tasted bad before they tasted it.

One of the things that was most interesting to me about gay male sexuality is that men want to learn it. They assumed that learning was a part of sexual desire. I know this is a generalization, but in some ways, just by going to the bars, by going to clubs and baths, whether or not you turned out to be a gay man who was primarily monogamous, you had an expanded idea of what was sexually visible and possible in the world, and you could try it out on yourself. Part of what I've always felt most sad about is the limitations of what I could see and what I could feel and smell and watch about how other women did it. Because there were so few places where I could watch other women do it and have it be acceptable.

Gayle: And now you're talking not just about the danger element but a kind of normalization.

Amber: Exactly. Both.

Gayle: One thing you're talking about is a way in which sex becomes a normal human activity—and not just sex as something you talk about in terms of your latest romantic escapade but actually seeing people doing it with genitals and fluids and props and lube and towels. That that's part of the normal vision of gay male social life. It's not something that's always cut off in a corner, put behind a curtain, or only discussed in the abstract or as romance.

I always thought it was really interesting that most people feel that if they were out having sex somewhere and they ran into someone they knew, from their bank or their church or their school or their office, they would just shrivel and die from the stigma and shame. Whereas there's a way in which if a gay guy is out at the baths and he runs into his lawyer or his doctor, it's "Hi." It's like running into this person at the movies or a ball game or restaurant. It's not a big deal, and that was very refreshing. It wasn't about danger. It was about detoxifying sex as an area of insanity and just making it a kind of part of life, and I always appreciated that.

Amber: When I was out doing political organizing, a lot of the only reference points for gay sexuality were clubs, and there was a lot of sex going on in them. Those were moments that were enormously revealing in the early days in clubs when it was prostitutes, drag queens, butch/femme, and faggots. You watched people have all different kinds of sexual moments and be in different sexual cultures. It was a gift.

That was where I first learned that you didn't have to be the person sitting next to you in the bar. You could be fascinated by it, but it wasn't a threat to your own personal sexual desires. That's also a legacy I inherited as a woman that I've had to really resist—the idea that other people's sexual pleasures and sexual engines were not necessarily my own. Just because they were doing it, I didn't somehow take on everything that they were doing with all its meaning. It took me a while to separate out my own imagination from my extraordinary interest, and guilt from desire.

Gayle: I guess I encountered gay male sexual culture later in my career as a lesbian than you did in yours, because I first came out in the context of a lesbian–feminist political environment. And I was in a small college town where there really wasn't much of a preexisting gay culture of any sort. I slowly worked my way into contact with larger, historically older gay and lesbian cultures. Then in the late 1970s, I actually did research on a gay male sexually defined population. At the time that was probably considered a complete leap into the abyss, but that's another story.

So I encountered gay male sexual culture in the late 1970s. For me, there was an enormous delight and wonder in it. It seemed a gift of a whole set of ways of thinking that I simply hadn't encountered before.

But Jewelle, you were referring to this earlier—the way in which men can think about having sexual pleasure as just something they expect to get in this world. It's like you expect to eat. You can expect to have sex. That doesn't mean that you should steal food to have food or that you should force people to have sex, but this is a human need and it's OK to fulfill it in some way. And there was an ease around it that I really appreciated.

One of the things that I got from gay male culture was ironic, given that the men I was mostly hanging around didn't much like women's bodies. They didn't like bodies like mine. And yet their ease with their own bodies made me feel better about my body and easier about being in a body. It was OK to have a body with holes and sphincters and fluids and sensations. And it was even OK to have a plump female body. You wouldn't think being involved with a group of men who were really into masculinity, muscle, and dicks would ever make you feel better about a female body. But in fact, it did because they were just willing to get naked and revel in their bodies as sources of pleasure. And it wasn't like everybody there was a calendar model or a body beautiful. There was this sense that bodies were just these wonderful things. You have a limited time with your body, and you should wring as much joy out of it as possible, and this was a perfectly legitimate pursuit. I found this attitude amazing.

Also, there was a way in which the set of available roles for expressing certain kinds of desires was expanded for me by encountering gay male culture. In lesbian culture, at that point in my life experience, I had run into mostly either butch/femme attitudes; that is, if you were butch, you were supposed to go out with a femme and you were supposed to run the sex. Or else it was the flannel-shirt-lesbian-feminist-hiking-boots mentality in which we all kind of looked the same, even though we all might have done different things. But this exhausted the available roles.

And none of them quite fit me because, for example, I've always been kind of a soft nerdy butch who just adored stronger and more masculine butches. There wasn't much of a framework for that in lesbian culture. But in gay male culture, there were all these frameworks for butch/butch sexuality and role models for being butch where you didn't ruin the sex. You could be a bottom and still be a butch, and you could go out with other butches. You didn't have to put on a dress to get fucked. You *could* put on a dress and get fucked. But you didn't *have* to.

My encounter with gay male sexual cultures expanded my notions of the possibilities and semantic arrangements for different kinds of desires and roles. But in order to assimilate this, I had to put away some of my own prejudices. I had to be ethnographic in my approach and set aside some of my own subjective responses.

Jewelle: Which were?

Gayle: Well, you know what Amber and Eric [Rofes] have called the "ick" factor. I do think there is a way in which many people who have strong sexual preference for one gender often have some kind of revulsion for the physical characteristics of the other. And certainly I had my own set of these things.

I remember when I first took the San Francisco Sex Information [SFSSI] training. At the beginning they do the Fuck-a-Rama. They show a hundred porn movies, at once, with every conceivable act.

Amber: Every sex act in every gender combination.

Gayle: It's a very interesting tactic to make people realize that sex comes in all these varieties. And of course everyone is disgusted by something they see in the Fuck-a-Rama. This is why they show it. It introduces you to sexual variety, so you won't make hasty judgments or assume that everyone has the same sexual tastes.

The hardest thing for me to look at were all the spurting, coming cocks. So what do I do? I go and decide to study a bunch of gay men who think spurting, coming cocks are the best thing on the planet. Their imagery is drenched with semen. And in fact, the clubs are drenched with semen. I had to take a step back from my immediate reaction.

The work didn't change my basic sexual orientation, but it certainly changed my attitude. My fantasy life is vastly enriched by all the imagery I saw. But as one person told me when I first started doing my work, fantasies are hungrier than bodies. That was a very liberating thing to hear. In this culture we have the idea that if we think about something and it turns us on, then we're supposed do it. And if it's something that we really don't want to do, we're in conflict with the fantasy. I realized that people have all kinds of fantasies. You can jerk off to them, but you don't have to go do all of those things.

Amber: I feel like I have a lot of sense of debt to gay male sexuality, for myself. And I've thought that for a long time. Some, because it protected me when I felt very different from a lot of lesbians around me. It was where I escaped to that was still gay. And . . . they just didn't care. They didn't care what I was into. It wasn't like a big deal if they didn't get it. It just wasn't judgmental in the same kind of way.

I had to work out my own sense of my sexuality and I needed a neutral place to do it, and the political part of my own community wasn't a helpful place for me. And in fact, it's true that the only time I've ever tried to commit suicide was when I had to try to deal with being a femme—not with trying to deal with being a lesbian. That was so dangerous in my own mind. Up against what I thought I should be, that desire looked so . . . it seemed so irreconcilable with my own political beliefs that I was just beside myself. Because I couldn't give up my erotic life, and I couldn't give up my political beliefs, and I couldn't bring the two together. And I couldn't keep living in different worlds for both of them. I don't want to make it sound like it was just lesbian feminism or something that did that, I was still in conflict about desire. And desire for what I wanted.

But the other part that I've recognized because of that femme identity, for which I feel an enormous sense of gratitude, is that my femme identity is profoundly influenced, and has been extraordinarily shaped by, drag. I never saw myself as a natural woman. I never ever believed in naturalness.

I wasn't a femme because I felt like I was a "real" woman. Which was kind of the ideology, right? The butches were "guys," and the femmes were "girls," real girls, which is part of why we were suspected of actually slipping over into the heterosexual camp, because we were "realer" in that sense. That femminess was "natural." So it wasn't as equally constructed as the identity of anyone else.

Jewelle: Right. As much based on play as butch was.

Amber: So I would look around and think, What women look like me to myself? I have always looked like a drag queen. I had always liked looking like a drag queen. And I've always been actually quite conflicted in how to not compete with drag queens.

Like in Cherry Grove, I was very careful, for instance, to not wear boas. Because I felt like I had an advantage that was both a limitation and a privilege in this culture. I had the biological body that was represented by men in drag.

Jewelle: You had tits, you didn't need the boa!

Amber: I had tits and I had cleavage and, hey. . . . And so it was very delicate to try and figure out how to respect drag queens and be a femme. How could I put those together? I didn't want to compete with them for being the prettiest girl. I didn't want to be more female than them.

They were who I saw myself as, as a woman. And so for me, that's the other place for gay male culture that's been unbelievably helpful. Because they also knew the irony of not being "real" girls. They knew that they were not girls like their mothers. And I am not a girl like my mother. I am not a femme like my mother, in all her conflict, has ever been a femme. And I'm always not quite the femme I would like to be.

I always feel like that's true around men in drag when you see them take off their wigs and kind of just walk down the street. Somewhere in that I also felt this part of me. There are places when I'm not that high femme. I don't look like what the expectation of myself is, for that piece, I'm not "real" enough.

And there was then a whole community of men, even if they didn't see me as part of them, which they didn't, but that I related to as also witty and brittle and bitchy and kick-ass. I mean, these were the men that I also saw defend themselves and other gay men in bars. These were not feminine images of passivity. These were women who defended their right to be in heels and defended their right to suck guys off and kicked butt when somebody attacked them. And so in many class ways, I also felt very connected to drag queens around my own sense of my own marginalization.

Jewelle: I'm not sure if what I learned from gay male sexuality isn't all intellectual gain. And certainly that's not to dismiss it because intellectual gain is really important.

I mean, I was thinking about your stories about the guys in drag and sort of following their lead, in a way, about how to be a woman. For me, as a femme, the people I was following were prostitutes. As a kid growing up, in the bars where my father and my stepmother worked, pimps and prostitutes were my aunts and uncles. And so as I became self-aware physically, I know I was patterning myself after these women, Miss Joanne and Miss Billy. . . . You know, the women who were like drag queens, larger than life. And so that's where I saw myself, in terms of attitude, physicality, independence. . . .

Amber: The right to desire.

Jewelle: I think I probably have a lot more of an intellectual debt to gay men. Starting with James Baldwin and the idea that desire could be hard-edged, immutable, and as Gayle said, you should be able to expect to have it fulfilled. And in reading and talking and listening to gay men.

Because I don't think I've had that many experiences in the gay male community. And the ones that I've had have always been tempered by my having to put aside my own feminist concerns in order to enjoy their company. Which I am capable of doing. But you know, whenever I have done organizing projects, if I work with a gay man for any length of time, I almost inevitably have to deal with misogyny, so I have tended to not have many extensive interactions, socially. So I think it's mostly intellectual.

Amber: What about gay male porn?

Jewelle: Oh, how much do I own?

Amber: That's one of the other places that I was thinking of that has really always been important to me. . . .

Jewelle: Yeah. That's true.

Amber: That was a place that was queer. I mean, I like straight porn. And I watch it. But lesbian porn, usually, was pretty—

Jewelle: It didn't exist until—

Amber: Didn't exist very much. Then a lot of it wasn't my stuff. It was boring. It was really flat. In fact, it was more like campy. You'd kind of sit there, and you wouldn't jerk off, you'd—

Gayle: Laugh off.

Amber: Exactly. If you wanted a place where you could play with desire and see all kinds of explicit sexualities and things happening, gay male porn was the other place for me of entry that I really, again, appreciated gay men for giving me space around.

Even though . . . I mean, often I think gay male culture has been for me in some ways like what I had to do around straight culture, when I had to change the gender of the person in the song. You know what I mean? I had to do some rearranging in there, but I was also very glad the song existed. And so a lot of times gay male culture has been like that for me. It's given me a gay place, even though I had to do some work.

Gayle: That creative spectatorship that doesn't require quite as much creativity as doing it with straight porn. And sometimes not as much conflict.

Jewelle: I don't have a real "ick" factor. I don't have things about men that I find "icky" physically. And I've certainly slept with enough men in my life that I know their bodies fairly well. So to me, male porn, gay male porn, has always been much more stimulating. Because it's just, it's all out there. And it gives you the chance to project yourself into homoerotic situations.

When I think about it, what were the shows I watched as an adolescent? *Star Trek* and *Route 66*. These were two shows whose homosocial qualities were what attracted me each week.

Gayle: No shit.

Jewelle: There was this intense subtext that I was projecting myself into. And with gay male porn, I could see myself . . . I was John Preston in some parts of my mind.

Amber: Thank you very much for the cuffs.

Gayle: I love gay male porn and see a lot of it. Because of my work, my house is filled with it. It's a running joke among my friends that I'm the dyke with the dick collection. They bring me penises. Someone even gave me an ocarina that you blow through the piss slit to get a sound out of it.

I wanted to say more about this history of lesbians appreciating gay male culture. It didn't just start recently. There's this idea that lesbians just discovered gay male culture in the last couple of years, and that isn't true. It's been going on a long time. Often until something is contextualized or written down or made into a movie, people think it doesn't exist.

Several years ago, Susie Bright wrote a piece on lesbians reading gay male porn for *On Our Backs.* The very first *Heresies* sex issue, from 1981, had an article about fag-hagging women. I'm sure there has been plenty of interaction and mutual learning for a long time.

I want to say some other things about influences of gay male sexual culture on lesbians. Certainly, in terms of S/M lesbians, gay men have been extremely important in that they had an S/M subculture when lesbians didn't. This doesn't mean that lesbians discovered S/M from gay men or wouldn't have done it without gay men or that they're only imitating gay men. But certainly gay men provided models for how to create an institutionalized subculture. There were also gay men who shared technical information with women. They had places to go buy toys or hold events. So gay men had an enormous impact on the emergence of the lesbian leather community. Without the assistance of gay leather men, it would have taken a lot longer and perhaps assumed different forms.

But I do want to disagree with the analysis that blames gay men for all the lesbian behavior that's considered reprehensible or politically incorrect by certain lesbian–feminist factions. Sheila Jeffreys exemplifies such views. I think that's an unfair, historically oversimplified, and condescending perspective. There's been a lot of influence back and forth. Lesbians have certainly influenced gay men, and gay men have certainly influenced lesbians for a long time. And that's not negative.

It doesn't mean that either culture is inauthentic. Cultures borrow all the time—that's the nature of culture. And it is certainly not unique to lesbians or gay men. People borrow and assimilate and retool ideas and artifacts and institutional formats from other cultures and use them for their own purposes. If there are "natural" parts of social life, that's certainly one of them.

Jewelle: Well, I'll jump in. I just want to put in one little thing about the expectations people have about the separation between lesbians and gays, certainly the separations between our perceptions about sex. And I had two sort of funny experiences. One was, I was on a panel with Samuel Delany who is certainly erudite, intelligent, and you know . . .

Amber: Queer.

Jewelle: Very queer. So we're on a panel, and at some point we were talking and I said, "Oh, Chip, I just wanted to tell you, I've been reading *Tides of Lust,* and God. . ." And Chip's eyes bugged open. It was like his *mother* had just told him she was reading *Tides of Lust.* And he recovered quite well, and he looked at me and he stroked his beard and just said, "Oh, really." That's very funny. And so I thought, "Have I just made Samuel Delany blush? Wow. Great." I said, "I'm glad I didn't go into detail about my reading of it."

Then recently, at a memorial reading for Essex Hemphill, at A Different Light bookstore, we all read from Essex's work. And I chose a very funny, explicitly sexual piece. And the store was packed, and I was reading it and I was loving it, and I would look out and see the mostly male audience look at me. . . . They were stunned.

Amber: That's what he would love. It was part of his work. That's part of what you can honor in his work.

Jewelle: It was clear that it was not being dragged out of me, that I had not been forced to read this, and that I was, in fact, enjoying it. And trying as hard as I could to read it with the same exuberance that Essex would. There's one funny line, something about his dick was so hard, he thought it was going to crack to pieces and fall to the floor or something.

Afterward, the guys who came up and spoke to me said, "Well, uh, you certainly read that well." I'm like, "I don't have a reading problem, what do they think?" Even though I don't necessarily spend a lot of time with gay men, certainly our cultures get things from each other. And the presumption that they don't is, I think, a mistake that sometimes both lesbians and gay men perpetuate.

Gayle: And it's also the case that although both lesbians and gay men have their separatists, not everybody in either community has always shared those views. Even separatists learn from one another in a more indirect way.

Amber: I would be interested to know what gay men thought they have learned, sexually, from us. The majority of gay men that I know, even if they think feminism is important, even if they value that part of the dialogue, they do not think that there's anything that's actually about their own desire represented in lesbian sexuality. I'm sure that's not true in S/M communities, but it is very true in other places. So, they just look at me like, "Why would I want to know what you do? Why would that be a conversation that would be interesting and informative about my desire?" Whereas I actually do feel like that, often, about gay male sexuality, even if I don't do it the way they do it. But then I'm interested in how people do it, anyway.

Jewelle: They have a much higher "ick" factor than you do, I think.

Amber: I just think that a lot of men that I know, gay men that I know, regardless of their passionate relationships with lesbians, their incredible friendships, the one area that they don't feel comfortable talking about and really getting into is how lesbians fuck. And I've found that particularly problematic around HIV, because the work I do is lesbian HIV work. And so it's been interesting to me that I have felt a need to defend things like issues of public sexuality and HIV as part of that debate, but they haven't felt a need to defend lesbian sexuality against state intervention or even know what it is.

And the idea that they could, as a normal part of their lives, say *clitoris,* or *vagina* as something that in an HIV context, they actually need to know, like I need to know about their desire and their practices and stuff—it astounds me every single, solitary day. I work in an AIDS organization that runs one of the major nonprofit AIDS hotlines, and when somebody calls to ask a question about HIV, until fairly recently the practice was that if it was a woman calling to ask about any kind of female sexuality, they would wait until they had a woman on the line to answer her question, regardless of what she was asking. And the assumption was that there wasn't anything men needed to learn or know about women's bodies and desires.

Jewelle: Is this not traditional in a male-dominated society? Gay men tend to be not any different from straight men in their unwillingness to know the female body more than superficially, whether it's dating or drag.

Amber: Well, I just don't know what it's from. I'm sure that's part of it, Jewelle. But given that I feel like I'm incredibly interested in their sexuality, because I really feel like it's information about my own—I mean, I see my connection to gay male sexuality. I feel like a lot of the themes of sexual desire are similar, even if the sexual practices are different. Like semen is not the same. . . . But my girlfriend fucks me and we talk about her cock getting hard. It's like an important piece of our lives. And it's amazing that there's nothing correspondingly interesting, intrinsically interesting to men, or worth investigating about my sexuality.

Gayle: If it's true that gay men are not interested in lesbian sex, is it because they think only penises have sex?

Amber: But least in my partnerships, one of us has a penis. But that's not even interesting to them.

Gayle: Now why do you think that's different among S/M folks?

Amber: My assumption is there is a lot more freedom to play with ideas of desire that cross gender.

Gayle: I do think that in leather and S/M communities, there is a lot of communication about sex. This is partly because the things that are sexualized are so much more numerous and varied than genitals and bodies. If you know how a tie a knot in a rope, you can show somebody else how to tie a knot in a rope, whether you're a woman or a man. There's this body of technical information and technique that's highly eroticized but does not have much to do with reproductive anatomy.

I also think there are certain common dynamics. There's been a lot of communication in leather communities in the last twenty years or so between women and men, gay, straight, bi, and transgendered, about mutual interests such as bondage, boot care, dungeon design, or relationship dynamics. For example, top burnout isn't gender specific. In S/M, there are areas where the genders can tend to fall away.

I think the bafflement about female sexuality tends to increase as sex gets more genitally focused. Some gay men just don't get what's happening with female bodies.

Jewelle: In contrast, what is biologically a physical manifestation of desire, since it is different, between male and female . . . in some cases, not so subtle, but in most cases, more subtle in female arousal than male. I think the manifestation of having a penis that is erect and solid and present that you hold onto outside the body. As I grip my hand this way, I remember how that feels. And a female's body, the arousal process is so different. So much of it is internal or about wetness, softness.

Granted, there are women who have clits that are hard as a rock. And I want their phone numbers. But—

Amber: I love you.

Jewelle: You know what I'm saying? It's like an "in" kind of thing. The sensation is kind of "in," as opposed to out and projectile and all that kind of stuff. So maybe that makes it so subtle that men can dismiss it.

Gayle: I'm going to argue the other side now. In the late 1970s when I first attended gay male fist-fucking parties, the guys were doing a lot of drugs and so often didn't get hard-ons. There would be a roomful of guys fisting, having a grand old time. There usually wasn't an erect penis to be found—at least until about three in the morning when the drugs started to wear off. The active sexual part were hands and holes. I saw a very male sexuality that was nonetheless oriented to orifices and arms. Before I went into this environment, I thought, "Oh, this is going to be very difficult. All these guys getting naked." And then I looked around, and it reminded me of lesbian sex.

Amber: You know one of the places I've consistently experienced problems with gay men around erotic identities is with gay men's hostility toward butches. It's really been interesting to me that often gay men liked feminine women, and femmes. But butch women, the more butch they were, the more stone they were, the more hostile.

Although I've seen some cruising. There have been crossovers. When Leslie and I were together, that was definitely true because men and women didn't know what gender she was, so it opened up the world of possibility. So a lot of gay men wanted to be fucked by her. And it was faggot to faggot. But they made her a faggot. They didn't make her a butch.

When I've been a femme alone, by myself around gay men, that's often been easier than when I've been with a very butch lover. Gay men had trouble trying to figure out how to treat the butch and see who she was. Was she a guy? Or was she a girl? And the gender has a lot of nuanced meanings in our own communities, both the lesbian communities and the gay male communities. It wasn't as though butches were seen as gay men by gay men, they were seen as somehow "other."

Gayle: Well, some of that may be erotic tension, some of it may be gender discomfort. And that may be a different issue.

Amber: Yeah. I think it's confusing because I think of butch as much as an erotic identity as a gender identity. But I wonder whether gay men see it as a gender threat.

Gayle: As an appropriation or as a gender confusion, perhaps? Some gay men are comfortable with gender crossing and gender confusion, but others are not. Just as some lesbians are.

Amber: What Gayle was talking about having fantasies that you didn't necessarily have to do—that's an idea that seems to me to be severely limited in this culture, even more severely limited for women. And that any place that you can break those lines, open up, can give you an opportunity to open up your own erotic imagination . . . even though you may use what you take in, very differently, from what the people doing it, you know, in front of you, mean it to be. It doesn't necessarily mean that what you do with what you see is literal. But what it does is give you more to draw on.

And I feel like one of the things that is most tragic in the culture in general—but for sure with women—is the lack of sexual repertoire and terrain . . . imaginative terrain for women. But that's been one of the ways that we've been most controlled, punished, and restricted in the culture.

Gayle: To some degree, I think that gay men in this culture, like straight men, tend to have a fairly narrow definition of what constitutes sexual attractiveness. There's a tendency to value certain body types, which are mostly young, thin, and/or muscular. One thing I like about lesbian sexual culture is that there truly is an appreciation of the beauty in a wider range of body types. There certainly is looks-ism among lesbians, as well, but there's also a very profound countertendency to celebrate a diversity of body type.

It's true that gay men have bears and chubby chasers, for example, but I think in general they tend to be more intolerant of people who are considered to be fat or overweight. And I wonder whether some gay men haven't picked up on the way lesbians value different physical types as something to appreciate. It's certainly something I love about lesbian culture.

Jewelle: Me, too. Me, too.

Amber: Thank God.

Gayle: There's also a distinction between appreciating diversity and sexually fetishizing particular types. There's a difference between a fetish and a kind of cultural norm that limits beauty to a very narrow range of acceptable bodies. I'm much less upset, for example, by a personal ad that specifies "I want a skinny butt" than I am by the notion that everyone should have a skinny butt.

Amber: I know the other area that really has been interesting to me about gay male sexuality that has really challenged my own thinking a lot, and that is how they organize relationships around sex. That they have a lot of different kind of arrangements around friendship and sexuality. That two men that are lovers can go someplace and each fuck other people.

Gayle: Lesbians do that, too. We just talk about it differently.

Amber: No, we break up over it.

Gayle: Not always.

Amber: But there's a cultural acceptance among men. The concept of betrayal usually is based on very different kinds of ideological assumptions, and a partner being sexual with someone else is not an assumption of betrayal or lack of commitment.

Those kinds of ideas, regardless of how I organized my own love life, challenged my thinking about how I wanted to think about commitment and about friendship and community. It just gave me some different ideas to work with. I think, especially because, much of the time, I have lived in a female world . . . that is what I've been both blessed with and what's been the problem. It was wonderful to have a whole other set of assumptions, whatever I wanted to take of them or not take of them, be operational.

So, you know, gay male friends of mine would look at me like, "Why would you break up with her because she slept with someone else?" Just incredulous about why I felt betrayal, for instance, or how I organized friendships. And that I thought friendships could never be sexual. And they would have these really fine distinctions between a fuck buddy, a lover, and a partner.

I really do struggle with this, and I struggle with it from a lot of different perspectives. I don't quite know what to do with the difference between what I need and what I believe. But it was a place that was helpful to me in recognizing how hurt I had been, young. That's the only way I can kind of think of it, that I carried a lot of baggage into my relationships with women that I then made look as though it was ideological.

Gay men helped me see that by showing me that other people who cared equally about being cared about and loved and sexual organized it very differently. Differently from me inside a lesbian community and differently from my mother and father. People were trying something else, and it wasn't just to be radical. And that some of the privilege of gender also allowed them to think about organizing relationships differently. And again, it was another place to breathe.

Gayle: I always wanted to organize relationships differently, but perhaps you're right. There is not as much precedent in lesbian culture, but there is some. For example, look at Natalie Barney, one of our lesbian foremothers, who believed in multiple simultaneous relationships, sleeping with her friends, and overcoming sexual jealousy.

Another example pertains to lesbian–feminist communities in the early seventies. There has been a lot of revisionist history portraying such communities as asexual or puritanical. The one I lived in was neither. It was a hotbed of passion, and there was also a politics that saw sexual jealousy as a manifestation of patriarchal property relationships. We argued against monogamy and the assumption that sex with others should break up couples.

Jewelle: Nonmonogamy was a good thing.

Gayle: Nonmonogamy was a crusade! There's a continuity in the slogans, from "Smash Monogamy" in the late 1960s, to "Monogamy is Monopoly" in the 1970s, to "Monogamy = Death" in the 1990s. There was a lot more variety in actual lesbian populations than the stereotypes would suggest. When I found gay men who actually had an institutionalized etiquette for nonmonogamy, it was a relief, but it was not all that different from my experiences in lesbian life.

Jewelle: I think it goes back to what you were saying earlier about normalizing sexual experience, putting it in the context of "This is acceptable and this is what we do, and—"

Amber: No big deal.

Jewelle: Right, right, which I think for lesbians has always been problematic. And will always be until we find ourselves, individually and as a group, less prey to the idea of ourselves as victims in the culture around our sex and sexual desire.

Gayle: And less subject to punitive measures for our sexuality.

Jewelle: Less subject to other people's vision of what we should be. I don't think I'd say it's healthier to use male models of sexual/emotional relationships. But the strength comes from feeling able to make a choice, based on our own desire.

Gayle: When women can have sex without losing their chance of economic security, without necessarily having to bear children, without losing their chances to go to school, without taking a lot of risks, then I think we'll have a different attitude toward it.

Jewelle: Having once had a conversation with a gay man about why I felt the lesbian and gay community, a particular organization of the community, should all come to a prochoice demonstration was like—

Amber: Swimming uphill.

Jewelle: It was. I kept saying, "But it is connected to women's sexuality. It is connected to your sexuality. Control of your own body. And women who decide to have sex with men are making a choice that puts them at risk. Because then do they have a baby? What do they do about that? Do they take birth control in order to not have babies and risk their health, long term?" And all of this. And it was really interesting for me to see a gay man totally unable to see the connection.

Gayle: Women have been dealing with the issue of "safer" sex for—

Everybody: A long time.

Gayle: That's why these things continue to be so important, not just for straight people, but for lesbians and gay men too. Without reproductive choice and good access to contraception and sex education, women are going to continue to be sexually disadvantaged in a very profound way. And it's also about educational opportunities and economic opportunities and more. . . . And some people think that's all a done deal and a done fight, that it's over. And they're totally wrong.

It is really about us: every single person on this planet who cares about sex in any way. We need to protect and expand reproductive rights and work for civil and economic conditions that make reproductive choice meaningful and possible. Many people don't realize how much even small gains around reproductive choice that were made years ago have now been systematically eroded. There are vast forces in this society continuing to try to raise the costs of sex for women, gay people, and young people of both genders.

Amber: And until the lesbian and gay male community see that as a fight about ourselves and our own sexuality and that the deepest meaning of sexual liberation is a very different autonomy, body autonomy, and sense of responsibility and instrumentality. And those things like reproductive rights are not somehow a "girl" thing or a child thing or any of that. They are at the heart of the battles that have been going on about HIV. They're often at the heart of ideas about "welfare cheats" and many of the kinds of ideologies that are so damaging to other cultures that are abused in this world. That those issues aren't somehow separated from their lives.

Jewelle: Who is defined as promiscuous, and whose promiscuity is defined as a problem?

Amber: And who is considered to put who else at risk around sexual desire? All those things.

Gayle: They're key issues right now.

Amber: For our survival.

CHAPTER 8

Slips

Roberto Bedoya, with Kaucyila Brooke and Monica Majoli

This project began as a search for images of lesbian sex created by gay male artists and of gay male sex created by lesbian artists. What I discovered was surprising: there were images of fag sex created by dykes but none the other way around. This absence became the impulse for Slips.

I've chosen the work of Los Angeles lesbian artists Monica Majoli and Kaucyila Brooke to accompany Slips. Majoli's work was created in 1990 and is part of her series of untitled paintings of gay male S/M scenes. These small oils on panels are based on stories that a gay friend told Majoli about his sexual encounters. Brooke's work is part of a collage series called *Tit for Twat: Can We Talk?* which uses the fotonovela form to create layered narratives about gender and sexual representation.

Monica Majoli, Untitled (oil, 1990).

Slips

is it the tongue
is it
sitting in panties
red, thinking of rita
hayworth, sipping tea
cultural crossing
of I lick, you lick
I bite, you bite
playing with pearls
dialogical encounters of the tongue

Monica Majoli, Untitled (oil, 1990).

the fag rhythm
the dyke rhythm

oscillations

the body knows
the thrill of being inside:
holes
whisper soft chiffon
gently fluted sides

tongues and will
that which asks of me

Monica Majoli, Untitled (oil, 1991).

(me of textures in like)
the pushing
the motor of exploration

in a touch

being touched
soft elasticated

lustrous body
suit
in ecstasies that transgress

rimming the
trace of the infinite as proximity
sex same
similar practices
in the intimate
fling of cunts and cocks

let's imagine
how do you picture and power
the play of limbs

the motions of desire
there
dis
covering the body
with
a tiny satin bow at front

speaking in tongues
outside Lick Observatory
probing gaze
beyond spectators and the world

questions in the hook of dreaming
slipping
under one's sense
shaped
desire to subjugate

imaging
twisted contorted figures
natural as
the body is frontier

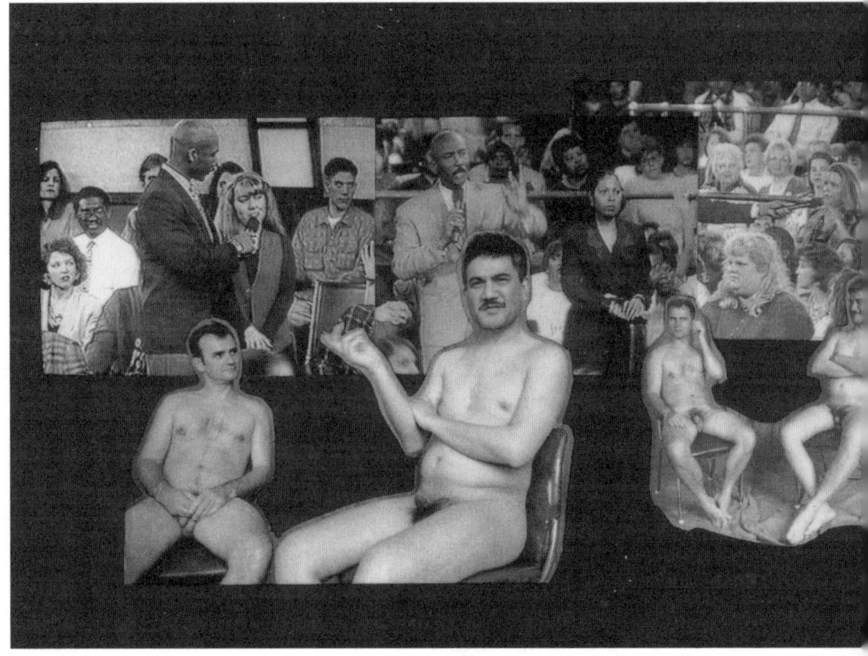

the horizon of nipple play
ruffled trimmed fingering

telling
narratives
fleshy muscular structures
diction, dialects
that, there
sheer
lingeries
to shape and smooth the story of bodies
filling it to taste

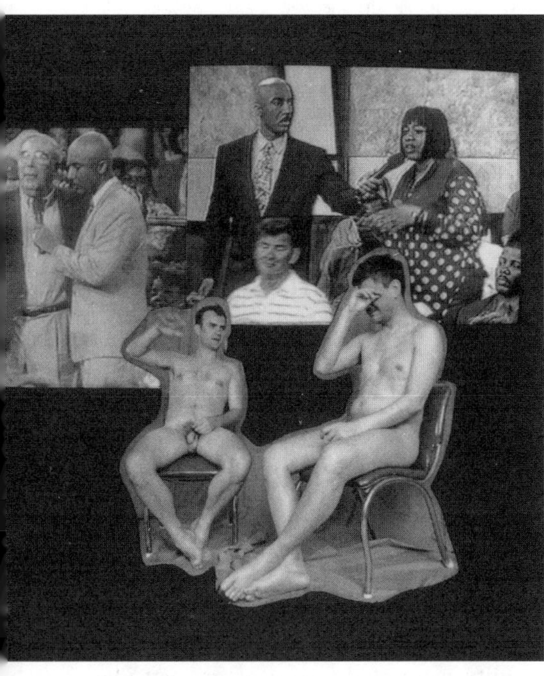

Kaucyila Brooke, detail from "Adam and Steve panels" from the project Tit for Twat: Can We Talk? *photomontage, original artwork in color, 1997.*

pliable
mix of tighten delights

tactile links
of
ones
figuring in tales of love
looks, counts in the eyes

How open is the mouth?

CHAPTER 9

Getting It Up for Politics: Gay Male Sexuality and Radical Lesbian Feminism

Robert Jensen

A while back I was describing my sexual orientation to a gay colleague, explaining that resistance to patriarchy and to the institutions of heterosexuality were at the core of my gay identity.[1] For me, being gay is as much about politics as desire, I explained.

He was intrigued, though a bit surprised. He said he had heard lesbians talk about the politics of choosing lesbianism but had never heard a gay man talk that way.

"And I think I know why," he said. "I've never known a man who could get it up for politics."

That comment goes to the heart of my struggle to understand my gayness and to fashion a sexual ethic for myself as a gay man. In politicizing questions about how we get it up and what we do with it once it is up, the work of radical lesbian feminists[2] has been central for me to defining a gay identity. This chapter identifies what I see as some of the key sexual issues for gay men and explains how radical feminism helps me work through them. While being careful not to extrapolate too wildly from my own experience, I argue that the depoliticized ideology of sexual liberation that is dominant in the gay community is inadequate for the formation of a healthy and coherent sexual ethic that seeks not only pleasure but also justice. The goal is not a "narrowing of sexuality at the margins" (Stychin 1995, p. 75) but, rather, a deepening of our understanding of sexuality at the margins and its role in progressive change.

Like many (if not most) gay men, I have struggled at various points in my life with self-doubt, confusion about desire, fear of gayness, and this culture's intense social pressure to live a heterosexual life.

Even though there is no "normal" route for gay men to an understanding of their sexuality, my own path has been different from that of most gay men I've talked with. By the time I understood myself as a gay man[3] and came out, I had been working for several years with the radical feminist critique of male sexuality, specifically the feminist critique of pornography (Jensen 1995a, 1995b, 1996). My first coherent thoughts about gay sexuality were framed by the radical lesbian feminists' politicization of sex rather than the depoliticization that commonly comes with a sexual liberationist ideology. I started on my gay path with a clear theoretical framework in which to question the eroticization of domination and submission and the implications for practices such as anonymous sex, anal sex, and the use of pornography, which I discuss later.

But although some aspects of my experience may be atypical, I do not believe the analysis I offer in this chapter is applicable only to my life. I argue that all gay men need to ponder the questions raised here, not because my resolution of them is the only one possible, but because the issues should not be avoided. One of the key lessons I have learned from feminism is that the personal is political and also that the political is personal; our analysis emerges from lived experience made visible through consciousness raising, and we must use this political analysis to shape our lives.

Many feminist activists and theorists have contributed to my understanding of heterosexuality, male sexuality, and male dominance (Cole 1989; Dworkin 1981, 1987, 1988, 1997; Frye 1983, 1992; Jeffreys 1990, 1993; MacKinnon 1987, 1989). There is, of course, much disagreement among feminists about sexuality, and it is important to note that the radical stance is only one viewpoint within feminism. But it is the viewpoint that resonates with my experience and provides what I believe is the most compelling interpretation of the world. In some academic circles, this kind of radical feminism is seen as passé, especially where postmodernism, queer theory, and sex-liberal politics are entrenched. Although my views on some issues have been influenced by postmodern critiques, it is important to me to make clear that this chapter and my politics are rooted in a radical feminist—and primarily a lesbian–feminist—view of the world. Here's my summary of that radical critique:

Sexuality and compulsory heterosexuality are key to the social subordination of women. As Marilyn Frye writes, for women to be subordinated and men to retain power, women

> must be reduced to a more-or-less willing toleration of subordination and servitude to men. The primary sites of this reduction are the sites of heterosexual relation and encounter—courtship and marriage-arrangement, romance, sexual liaisons, fucking, marriage, prostitution, the normative family, incest and child sexual assault. It is on this terrain of heterosexual connection that girls and women are habituated to abuse, insult, degradation. (Frye 1992, p. 130)

At their core, the sexual norms of patriarchy eroticize domination and submission. Men in contemporary American culture are commonly trained to view sex as the acquisition of physical pleasure through the taking of women. Sex is a sphere in which men believe themselves to be naturally dominant and women naturally passive. Women are objectified, and women's sexuality is commodified; women become a thing to be fucked, fucking that easily can be purchased (for example, by paying for dinner or buying a prostitute) or taken by force if necessary. Sex is sexy because men are dominant and women are subordinate—power is eroticized.

Summed up by Coveney and others (1984), the characteristics of "normal" heterosexual male sexuality are power (the need to dominate), aggression (from the subtle to the overtly violent), penis orientation (sex is defined by penetration by a penis), separation of sex from loving emotion, objectification (sexual partners require neither respect nor sensitive understanding), fetishism (women are eroticized as body parts), and uncontrollability (men must have sex when they feel aroused).

Pornography is one of the key sites in which these sexual values are reflected, reinforced, and normalized in contemporary culture. Domination and subordination are sexualized, sometimes in explicit representations of rape and violence against women, but always in the objectification and commodification of women and their sexuality (Dworkin 1981, 1988; MacKinnon 1987, 1993). This results in several kinds of harms to women: (1) the harm caused in the production of pornography, (2) the harm in having pornography forced on them, (3) the harm in being sexually assaulted by men who use pornography, and (4) the harm in living in a culture in which pornography reinforces and sexualizes women's subordinate status (Dworkin and MacKinnon 1988, pp. 41–52).

In a world in which men hold most of the social, economic, and political power, the result of the patriarchal sexual system is widespread violence, sexualized violence, sexual violence, and violence by sex against women, children, and, in certain situations, vulnerable men. This includes physical assault, emotional abuse, and rape by family members and acquaintances as well as strangers. Along with the experience of violence, women and children live with the knowledge that they are always targets. Sometimes in this system, men—most notably gay men—can be labeled "sissies," treated like women, and subjected to similar kinds of violence. This analysis is not intended to suggest that every man is a rapist in legal terms but that we live in a society in which men, both legally designated rapists and nonrapists, are typically taught rapist ethics (Stoltenberg 1989); men are raised with a view of women and sex organized around status, hostility, control, and dominance (Beneke 1982).

My experience and research indicate that the primary sexual lesson for boys growing up in a patriarchy in the United States is simple: Fuck women. The details vary depending on the teacher. Some say, "Fuck as many women as often as you can for as long as you can get away with it." Others say, "Fuck a lot of women until you get tired of it, and then find one to marry and fuck just her." And others say, "Don't fuck any women until you find one to marry, and then fuck her for the rest of your life and never fuck anyone else." Most say, "Only fuck women." A few say, "Fuck other men if you want to."

The basic concepts are clear: Sex is fucking. Fucking is penetration. The things you do before you penetrate are just warm-up exercises. If you don't penetrate, you haven't fucked, and if you haven't fucked, you haven't had sex (Frye 1992, pp. 109–119). And if you aren't having sex, you're in trouble. Perhaps the most important rule of sex in a patriarchy is: You gotta get it. You have to fuck something at some point in your life. If you don't get it, there's something wrong with you. You aren't normal. You aren't really alive. You certainly aren't a man.

Because the object of gay desire is the male body, not the female, it is tempting to dismiss this feminist critique as not applicable to gay men (Sherman 1995; Tucker 1990a). Yet in many ways, gay and straight men are not radically different in the way they are socialized to understand and practice sex. The feminist critique of sexuality can be useful in analyzing gay culture because straight and gay men are raised with the same default sexual values normalized in patriarchy: sex as the acquisition of physical pleasure from another, sex as the exercise of power over others, sex as disconnected from intimacy and affection toward another.

In other words, straight and gay men may have more in common when it comes to sex and sexual politics than is commonly assumed (Stanley 1982). Frye suggests that gay men and lesbian feminists often find themselves at odds politically because gay men remain loyal to patriarchal constructions of masculinity and male supremacy:

> The general direction of gay male politics is to claim maleness and male privilege for gay men and to promote the enlargement of the range of presumption of phallic access to the point where it is, in fact, absolutely unlimited. The general direction of lesbian feminist politics is the dismantling of male privilege, the erasure of masculinity, and the reversal of the rule of phallic access, replacing the rule that access is permitted unless specifically forbidden with the rule that it is forbidden unless specifically permitted. (Frye 1983, p. 145)

For me, being gay means not only acknowledging sexual desire for men but also resisting the norms and practices of patriarchy. Gayness is not only about what I do, with whom, with my body. It also is about a set of political choices involving a conscious attempt to disconnect from heterosexual norms and patriarchy. Such a commitment is difficult to make good on in a world of male privilege, and I have found few role models for how to live ethically as a man—straight or gay—in a patriarchy.[4] Frye argues that if a gay man rejects patriarchy, he will have to do what lesbian feminists have been doing all along: invent.

> He has to invent what maleness is when it is not shaped and hardened into straight masculinity, gay hypermasculinity or effeminacy. For a man even to begin to think such invention is worthwhile or necessary is to be disloyal to phallocracy. For a gay man, it is to be the traitor to masculinity that the straight men always thought he was. (Frye 1983, p. 146)

This chapter is part of that process of invention, my ongoing attempt to find ways to understand how patriarchal norms live in me and to devise strategies for change. Again, I do not have definitive answers; my goal is not to dictate a single correct position but to be part of a conversation in which we need not be afraid of making political and moral judgments about sexual practices.

In a world in which the expression of love and desire for a person of the same sex can be punished by anything from a demeaning remark to a violent attack, sensitivity to attempts to talk about sexual norms, even in our own communities, is understandable. When in the dominant culture we are labeled diseased, deviant, immoral, and generally less than fully human because of the imposition of heterosexuality as a norm, an aversion to sexual rules in general can seem sensible.

Hence, the prevailing norm among many gay men often seems to be "anything goes." Even if a man doesn't make certain practices a part of his own sex life, the understanding is that the practices are not to be critiqued, especially not in public. I am not suggesting that the gay community is monolithic, but the majority of the gay men I talk to do, to some degree, endorse this stance. In my experience, the sexual liberationist ideology—the idea that whatever anyone finds sexually pleasurable is, by definition, good—is rarely challenged in gay culture. To question any gay sex practice is to risk being accused of the worst of sins: sex phobia and prudery, moral authoritarianism, and internalized homophobia.

Those of us who want to subject sex to a political and moral analysis are often accused of seeking to repress sexual desire out of a fear of the wildness of sex, of trying to tame the untamable, of attempting to turn away from the transgressive nature of sex. But the question of repression can, and should, be turned around: Do sexual libertarians repress a nagging fear that politicizing sex practices might force them to ask difficult questions about their own sex lives or to consider the possibility that new ways of being physically intimate need to be found? If the rule of sex in patriarchy is "you gotta get it" and a political analysis of sex leaves open the possibility that how we have learned to "get it" might have to be modified, then we have to face the question of whether "getting it" might have to be put on hold while we work through the politics.

I return to this issue at the end of the chapter, but for now I want to point out that the "anything goes" position is a political and moral stance, not the absence of a stance. To refuse to examine the political and moral questions surrounding sex is to endorse a certain politics and morality. There are political and ethical implications in all aspects of everyday life—the decisions to drive cars, eat certain kinds of foods, buy certain kinds of products, and so forth—including sex. There is no escape from judgment, nor should we seek such an escape. To be human is to ask these questions. Do we ask them honestly, with a commitment to justice, without turning away from those questions that are difficult?

This chapter focuses on gay male sexual practices. It is directed specifically to gay men and not the debate over the sexual practices of lesbian, bisexual, or heterosexual women. Many of the issues I discuss here are relevant to women, but that analysis is not my project. I am aware, for example, that many lesbians would reject the radical analysis of sexuality and endorse some of the practices I critique.

The focus of much of the debate in the so-called lesbian sex wars has been on sadomasochism (for early critiques and defenses, see Linden et al. 1982; SAMOIS 1982). Although sadomasochism perhaps raises questions about the sexualization of domination and submission more clearly than other sexual practices do, my guess is that the time spent discussing it is disproportionate to the frequency of its practice. Instead, in this chapter, I want to concentrate on sexual practices that are likely more common among gay men.[5]

To say that anonymous sex, anal sex, and the use of pornography are gay male sex practices is not to say that all gay men participate in them or that they define being gay. It is simply to acknowledge that they are widespread and, in many gay circles, not challenged even if not embraced. I contend, however, that all three practices need to be challenged and that the radical feminist critique of sexuality provides a useful framework for that project.

Because they are outside heterosexuality, all gay sex practices are sometimes taken to be inherently radical and resistant to conventional heterosexual norms. People who object to these gay practices are often said to be trying to mimic heterosexuality by denying the inherently transgressive nature of gay sex. But it is these practices themselves that mimic heterosexuality in their acceptance of patriarchal sexual values: the disconnection of sex from affection and emotional interaction with another, the heterosexual equation of sex with penetration and domination and submission, and the commodification of sex in pornography. There is little that is radical about these practices; they serve mainly to reinforce patriarchal notions about sex.

Anonymous Sex

A gay friend once reported to me, "My sex life is great, but my love life stinks." He meant that he was getting adequate sexual satisfaction through casual and anonymous sex partners he picked up but that he felt something missing in his emotional life. The common dissociation of sex from emotion by men in patriarchy made his comment not only understandable but unexceptional. Such a severing of sex and loving affection is not universal among gay (or straight) males, but it is also not unusual. In a system that views sex as the acquisition of pleasure, anonymous sex is a perfectly plausible way, perhaps even the preferred way, of obtaining sexual gratification. But does such sex provide the human connection that we seek in our erotic lives?

I ask that question well aware that certain practices—anonymous sex in parks, bathrooms, and pornographic bookstores, for example—are connected to historical conditions of oppression. Gay men who, for whatever reasons, do not live openly gay lives have sought sexual connections in this fashion, and I do not intend a mean-spirited or harsh judgment of such choices. I am familiar with such feelings; one of my gay sexual experiences as a young man began with a bookstore pickup. That does not mean, however, that the issue cannot be discussed or the practice critiqued. To acknowledge that a practice was forced on us by history does not mean we must continue to defend it. As I argue, if anonymous sex reinforces patriarchal sexual norms, then closeted gay men face the same choices that out gays do, even if the circumstances are different and the choices more difficult. Also, anonymous sex practices are hardly restricted to closeted men (Browning 1993, pp. 74–79), as to some degree they have been institutionalized in the commercial sex industry's bathhouses and sex clubs (Young 1995). This issue is crucial, therefore, to the whole gay community.

To raise questions about anonymous sex and promiscuity is not to endorse mainstream heterosexual dictates about monogamy. Promiscuous gay sex is often set off against monogamous heterosexual sex, as if the two were somehow inherently opposed. On one level, of course, the generalizations are false: Many gay men are not promiscuous, and many straight men are not monogamous. But beyond that, in patriarchy, promiscuity and monogamy are not necessarily in opposition but are more like flip sides of a coin. The important question is not the number of sexual partners but how one has sex. A married heterosexual man can have sex with his wife in a manner that treats her as nothing more than a fuck object, just as a gay man can enter the bushes in a park and engage in sex with a stranger in the same fashion. For many men (gay and straight), life includes both a period of promiscuity (in which the goal is to fuck as many as possible) and monogamy (in which the goal is to fuck only one, although often with the possibility of illicit fucking on the side, kept out of view and hence made more exciting). I argue that even though there is no guarantee that sex in a monogamous relationship moves beyond that, anonymous sex is patriarchal sex and is incompatible with resistance to patriarchy.

Anal Sex

A friend who volunteered on an AIDS hotline once told me that in addition to questions about transmission of the virus, many of the men who called were interested in talking about their sex lives more generally. It was not unusual, he said, for men to admit that they used their fear of AIDS as a justification for not engaging in anal sex, about which they had always been ambivalent anyway. In other cases, especially with younger gays, it had never occurred to them that they could say no to anal sex, that the practice was viewed as constitutive of being gay, a notion my friend would gently question. This experience suggests that a more open conversation is needed in the gay community about what penetration means in this culture.

Again, this discussion does not assume that every gay man participates in anal sex. Rofes (1996, p. 178), citing surveys that show that from 10 percent to 50 percent of gay men do not engage in anal sex, conservatively estimates the figure at 20 percent, based on his experience as a gay activist and in AIDS organizations. My experience is that gay men who reject anal sex explain it as a personal choice, something they just don't like. My goal is to frame it as a political issue, not solely a matter of personal preference.

Attention to the meaning of the principal male slang term for sexual intercourse—*fuck*—is instructive. To fuck a person is to penetrate him or her. To fuck someone in another context ("he really fucked me over on that deal") means to hurt or cheat someone. When hurled as a simple insult ("fuck you"), the intent is denigration, and the remark is often prelude to violence or the threat of violence. People continue to use the same word for sex and aggressive or violent behavior, even though there is great resistance to the notion that sex as fucking is linked to domination, aggression, and violence. The linguistic practice suggests that we need to reflect critically on the sexual practice, which lesbian feminists have long done. For example, Andrea Dworkin writes: "The normal fuck by a normal man is taken to be an act of invasion and ownership undertaken in a mode of predation; colonializing, forceful (manly) or nearly violent; the sexual act that by its nature makes her his" (Dworkin 1987, p. 63). If one accepts that claim—even if only for the sake of argument here—

the question remains whether the shift from a man's penetration of a woman to his penetration of another man changes the meaning of intercourse. Also, does the fact that men can switch from being penetrated to being the one who penetrates change the nature of the act? Or does intercourse, as it is shaped by and practiced in a patriarchy, require that the person being penetrated (man or woman) be subordinate? Can the social meaning of intercourse, constructed over a long period of time and deeply rooted in the culture, be subverted by individuals seeking to change the meaning of the practice?

My own assessment is that at this point I could not practice anal sex and resist patriarchal sexual norms. Some men who practice anal sex say that having a man inside them or being inside a man does not engender feelings of domination and submission but instead a sense of intimacy, trust, and closeness (Rofes 1996, pp. 146–147). I am not suggesting that such men are the victims of false consciousness, and I do not ignore their experiences. Furthermore, I am not suggesting my assessment is the only reasonable one, only that the meaning of anal sex should be a central issue in discussions of gay male sex.

Pornography

Many gay writers and critics view pornography as a site of resistance to heterosexual norms, a place to celebrate gay sexuality (Burger 1995; Tucker 1990b). In my experience, few gay men believe that the feminist critique of heterosexual pornography offers any insight into gay pornography. The most common responses I get to this idea are overt hostility or a lack of interest in the subject.

The feminist critique argues that one of the key messages in pornography is the eroticization of dominance and submission. In heterosexual pornography, this message most often takes the form of male control over, and abuse of, women. But the same eroticization of power can exist in a same-sex relationship. Whether top and bottom are male–female or male–male, the result is the same: Sex is about power and control.

Christopher Kendall argues that much like heterosexual pornography, gay male pornography glorifies conventional notions of the masculine and reinforces a male–female dichotomy that hurts women and gay men. He suggests that in gay pornography,

> assertiveness is linked with aggression, strength equated with violence, physical power and the right to overpower; intimidation, control of others, lack of mutuality and disrespect, and being hurt are presented as pleasurable; violating and being violated are presented as identity politics; and aggressive, non-consensual behavior is advanced as normal, liberating and sexually promoted as such. (Kendall 1993, p. 32)

Even in regard to pornographic magazines and videos that do not overtly eroticize domination, it is important to ask what kind of sex gay pornography offers us. In pornography, sex is turned into a commodity. Pornography gives us sex in which people are routinely used simply as fuck objects, sex in which all that matters is the generation of sufficiently exciting images to facilitate masturbation and produce an orgasm. In other words, pornography offers us sex that normalizes patriarchal values.

Clearly, gay male pornography is condemned in the wider society mainly because it is a tangible representation of life outside heterosexuality, and in that sense it is transgressive. But at what cost to gay culture and gay men? In all these arenas, it is possible on the surface to transgress norms yet reinforce those norms at a deeper level. To argue against pornography is not to claim that sexually explicit media have some extraordinary power by themselves to shape gay or straight life. But we cannot turn away from what pornography tells us about gay life.

Reasonable questions after such a critique might include (1) If these practices are problematic, what should gay men do with each other sexually? (2) If lesbian–feminist politics are useful to a critique, how can lesbian–feminist sex practices help guide gay men in figuring out something new? As my answers emerge in the rest of this chapter, it will become clear I am not at all sure that these are the right questions.

Frye writes in her essay "Lesbian 'Sex' " that after looking at a sex manual for gay men, she noticed that gay male sex is "articulate," that gay men have words for a wide variety of acts and activities. Lesbians, she suggests, are inarticulate: "I have, in effect, no linguistic community, no language, and therefore in one important sense, no knowledge" (Frye 1992, p. 115).

I can understand her concern that men's meanings have taken from women the ability to express themselves, but at another level I think the inarticulateness, at least in this particular historical moment, could be an advantage. In a pornographic culture, it is difficult to talk about sex in a way that does not become pornographic. That doesn't mean I believe there should not be talk about sex—after all, this chapter and much of my other work is about sex. The question is, What kind of talk about sex do we need right now? How should we talk about it?

One reason I have been drawn to radical lesbian–feminist work is that it discusses sex without being pornographic; it is a place I can go to work through issues free from that talk.[6] Again, this doesn't mean this work avoids sexual issues. But I tend to look for inspiration from work that deals with sex in its political context and searches for nonpornographic imagery. Poetry is often particularly helpful in this quest to see our "bodies entire" (Rukeyser 1978, p. 493; for other examples, see Cardea 1993, p. 242; Chrystos 1993, pp. 19–20; Rich 1978, p. 32).

I am suggesting that what gay men can take away from reading and talking with lesbian feminists is not a how-to manual on how to touch each other or what to do with our penises, hands, and mouths but insight into what sex means in patriarchy and how one can resist patriarchy, and a sense of what kind of connections lie beyond that. This critique leads me away from certain practices, but it does not provide me with a sexual cookbook. More important, the radical lesbian critique has led me to ask difficult questions about what sex practices mean and why power is central to the process of making them mean something. What is possible for me as I engage in this reflection about sex (at both a personal and a cultural level) leads me to a central question about the role of sex for me at this moment in history.

In challenging certain gay male practices, I am asking us to ponder: What is sex for? The question is crucial and cannot be dismissed with a libertarian wave of the hand.

For me, sex is about more than the pursuit and acquisition of physical stimulation and pleasure. Acquisitive sex turns me away from wholeness and connection; it requires the severing of mind, body, and emotion. I believe there is an essential connection among sex, compassion, and intimacy that is possible only when equality is eroticized. I reject the notion that power (in the sense of power over others) provides the sexiness of sex. The power I seek is power in relation to others, a movement away from the hierarchy of top and bottom and toward mutuality (Heyward 1989).

Central to this notion of sex is an expansion of our notion of the erotic. Audre Lorde's discussion of erotic power touches on many of these concerns. She talks about the way in which women's erotic power is falsely cordoned off in the bedroom, made into "plasticized sensation," and confused with the pornographic (Lorde 1984, p. 54). For Lorde, the erotic is a life force, a creative energy: "those physical, emotional, and psychic expressions of what is deepest and strongest and richest within each of us, being shared: the passions of love, in its deepest meanings" (Lorde 1984, p. 56).

Lorde writes about expressing her erotic power in some ways that the culture does not define as sexual and others that the culture might call sexual; she writes about the erotic power flowing both in the act of writing a good poem and in "moving into sunlight against the body of a woman I love" (Lorde 1984, p. 58). When the discussion of sexuality is expanded in this fashion, I find it easier to move away from the limiting patriarchal definition of sex as fucking.

A metaphor may help. There is a cliché that when an argument is of little value, it produces "more heat than light." One of the ways the mainstream culture talks about sex is in terms of heat: She's hot, he's hot, we had hot sex. Sex is bump-and-grind; the friction produces the heat, and the heat makes the sex good. Fucking produces heat. Fucking is hot.

But what if our embodied connections could be less about heat and more about light? What if instead of desperately seeking hot sex, we searched for a way to produce light when we touch? What if such touch were about finding a way to create light between people so that we could see ourselves and each other better? If the goal is knowing ourselves and each other like that, then what we need is not heat but light to illuminate the path.

How do we touch and talk to each other to shine that light? I am not always sure. There are lots of ways to produce light in the world, and some are better than others; moral and political considerations are relevant. Sunlight is better than light generated by fossil fuels; light that draws its power from rechargeable solar cells is better than light that draws on throwaway batteries. Likewise, there are lots of ways to imagine sex that transcends patriarchal norms. Some are better than others, depending on the values on which they are based. Our task is not necessarily imagining new ways of touching but always being attentive to the ethics and politics of the touch.

Given my notions of what sex is for, influenced by the radical lesbian–feminist critiques, I find myself striving to live out a sexual ethic that moves away from practices rooted in patriarchy.

One of the impediments to such progress, I believe, is the imperative to fuck, the idea that not to be sexually active is somehow to be not fully alive. It is tempting to rush toward new sexual practices before we have fully understood and abandoned patriarchal ones, but it may be that the process of inventing a nonpatriarchal gay sexuality requires a period of no sex, of human connection and intimacy that do not take traditional sexual forms. A Southern Women's Writing Collective (1990, p. 145) calls this process for women "deconstructive lesbianism," which has as its goal to deconstruct or dismantle sexuality at the personal and experiential level, "to unweave the pattern of dominance and submission which has been incarnated as sexuality in each of us." They call for a "radical celibacy" that "understands that sex has to stop before male supremacy will be defeated" (A Southern Women's Writing Collective 1990, p. 146).

I believe the development of a healthy, nonpatriarchal gay male sexual ethic also depends on ending male supremacy. Radical celibacy may be, for some of us, part of the path toward that goal. Others may explore new ways of sexual interaction. Different histories and life experiences, different emotional profiles, and different social locations mean that there will be many paths. My goal is to be part of a conversation that is respectful, honest, and unafraid of confronting the ethics and politics of our choices.

The immediate task may not be so much the exploration of specific sex practices but the creation of the conditions in which such explorations might go forward. It seems to me that such an idea—the work of creating a world in which sex and justice are not in conflict—could be a source of much passion and excitement as we move forward.

Notes

1. Parts of this chapter draw on ideas developed in an essay aimed more specifically at a heterosexual male audience (Jensen 1997).

2. I use this term to describe a group of writers, theorists, and activists who critique the institution of heterosexuality, pornography, and the eroticization of domination and submission. References to "the radical lesbian–feminist critique" throughout this chapter are meant to describe this perspective, which I summarize. Although I realize that other women with differing views might also claim the label of radical, I am following conventional typologies of different feminist perspectives (for example, Tong 1989) as well as indicating my view of which approach to feminism offers a truly radical critique.

3. People sometimes ask why I do not describe myself as bisexual. Although I have no aversion to the term, it does not describe how I feel about myself at this point in my life. My preference for the label gay is a mix of politics, desire, and emotion.

4. One exception I would like to make special note of is my partner Jim Koplin. Woven throughout this essay are the threads of several years of conversation with him about these issues.

5. These assertions are based on my sense of the gay world in the contemporary United States, not on systematic surveys. There is no reliable data that indicate how often gay men engage in certain practices, and even if such data existed, I would be skeptical of them given the methodological problems in such work.

6. Much lesbian writing is explicitly sexual and—both to me and to the authors—pornographic (for example, Califia 1988). Without venturing into a discussion of lesbian pornography, I want to acknowl-

edge that I am aware that I am drawing on only one segment of lesbian work on sex.

References

Beneke, Timothy. 1982. *Men on Rape.* New York: St. Martin's Press.

Browning, Frank. 1993. *The Culture of Desire.* New York: Random House.

Burger, John R. 1995. *One-Handed Histories: The Eroto-Politics of Gay Male Video Pornography.* New York: Harrington Park Press.

Califia, Pat. 1988. *Macho Sluts.* Boston: Alyson Publications.

Cardea, Caryatis. 1993. *Tremors.* In Julia Penelope and Susan J. Wolfe, eds., *Lesbian Culture: An Anthology,* pp. 240–242. Freedom, Calif.: Crossing Press.

Chrystos. 1993. *Lesbian Air.* In Mona Oikawa, Dionne Falconer, Rosamund Elwin, and Ann Decter, eds., *Out Rage,* pp. 19–20. Toronto: Women's Press.

Cole, Susan G. 1989. *Pornography and the Sex Crisis.* Toronto: Amanita.

Coveney, Lal, Margaret Jackson, Sheila Jeffreys, Leslie Kay, and Pat Mahony. 1984. *The Sexuality Papers: Male Sexuality and the Social Control of Women.* London: Hutchinson.

Dworkin, Andrea. 1981. *Pornography: Men Possessing Women.* New York: Perigee.

Dworkin, Andrea. 1987. *Intercourse.* New York: Free Press.

Dworkin, Andrea. 1988. *Letters from a War Zone.* London: Secker & Warburg.

Dworkin, Andrea. 1997. *Life and Death.* New York: Free Press.

Dworkin, Andrea, and Catharine A. MacKinnon. 1988. *Pornography and Civil Rights: A New Day for Women's Equality.* Minneapolis: Organizing against Pornography.

Frye, Marilyn. 1983. *The Politics of Reality.* Freedom, Calif.: Crossing Press.

Frye, Marilyn. 1992. *Willful Virgin.* Freedom, Calif.: Crossing Press.

Heyward, Carter. 1989. *Touching Our Strength: The Erotic as Power and the Love of God.* San Francisco: Harper & Row.

Jeffreys, Sheila. 1990. *Anticlimax: A Feminist Perspective on the Sexual Revolution.* New York: New York University Press.

Jeffreys, Sheila. 1993. *The Lesbian Heresy.* North Melbourne: Spinifex.

Jensen, Robert. 1995a. "Men's Lives and Feminist Theory." *Race, Gender & Class* 2: 111–125.

Jensen, Robert. 1995b. "Pornographic Lives." *Violence against Women* 1: 32–54.

Jensen, Robert. 1996. "Knowing Pornography." *Violence against Women* 2: 82–102.

Jensen, Robert. 1997. "Patriarchal Sex." *International Journal of Sociology and Social Policy* 17: 91–115.

Kendall, Christopher N. 1993. "Real Dominant, Real Fun!": Gay Male Pornography and the Pursuit of Masculinity." *Saskatchewan Law Review* 57: 21–58.

Linden, Robin Ruth, Darlene R. Pagano, Diana E. H. Russell, and Susan Leigh Star, eds. 1982. *Against Sadomasochism: A Radical Feminist Analysis.* East Palo Alto, Calif.: Frog in the Well Press.

Lorde, Audre. 1984. *Sister Outsider.* Freedom, Calif.: Crossing Press.

MacKinnon, Catharine A. 1987. *Feminism Unmodified: Discourses on Life and Law.* Cambridge, Mass.: Harvard University Press.

MacKinnon, Catharine A. 1989. *Toward a Feminist Theory of the State.* Cambridge, Mass.: Harvard University Press.

MacKinnon, Catharine A. 1993. *Only Words.* Cambridge, Mass.: Harvard University Press.

Rich, Adrienne. 1978. *The Dream of a Common Language: Poems 1974–77.* New York: Norton.

Rofes, Eric. 1996. *Reviving the Tribe: Regenerating Gay Men's Sexuality and Culture in the Ongoing Epidemic.* Binghamton, N.Y.: Haworth.

Rukeyser, Muriel. 1978. *The Collected Poems of Muriel Rukeyser.* New York: McGraw-Hill.

SAMOIS. 1982. *Coming to Power: Writings and Graphics on Lesbian S/M.* Boston: Alyson Publications.

Sherman, Jeffrey G. 1995. "Love Speech: The Social Utility of Pornography." *Stanford Law Review* 47: 661–705.

A Southern Women's Writing Collective. 1990. "Sex Resistance in Heterosexual Arrangements." In Dorchen Leidholdt and Janice G. Raymond, eds., *The Sexual Liberals and the Attack on Feminism*, pp. 140–147. New York: Pergamon.

Stanley, Liz. 1982. " 'Male Needs': The Problems of Working with Gay Men." In Liz Stanley, *On the Problem of Men*. London: Women's Press.

Stoltenberg, John. 1989. *Refusing to Be a Man*. Portland, Ore.: Breitenbush.

Stychin, Carl F. 1995. *Law's Desire: Sexuality and the Limits of Justice*. London: Routledge.

Tong, Rosemarie. 1989. *Feminist Thought: A Comprehensive Introduction*. Boulder, Colo.: Westview.

Tucker, Scott 1990a. "Gender, Fucking, and Utopia." *Social Text* 27: 3–34.

Tucker, Scott. 1990b. "Radical Feminism and Gay Male Porn." In Michael S. Kimmel, ed., *Men Confront Pornography*, pp. 263–276. New York: Crown Books.

Young, Ian. 1995. *The Stonewall Experiment: A Gay Psychohistory*. London: Cassell.

C H A P T E R 10

Through the Looking Glass: A Folsom Street Story

Mimi McGurl and Richard Schimpf

MM: All-male environments have always simultaneously intrigued and frustrated me. When I was a child, it seemed extremely unfair that girls like me were not allowed in the boys' club. Once I found my place in the community of women instead of men, my relationships with men became singular, and groups of men represented only a feeling of curiosity and exclusion. Talking for three years now with my friend Richard about his experiences at gay male sex clubs in San Francisco has reminded me of this old feeling. These are places I cannot go and could never imagine on my own.

RS: Mimi is more queer boy than she knows. She responds deeply to what makes men into queer boys: a shift in the moment that happens in these stories when your upbringing falls away. Mimi has heard most of my stories, and there are several that she particularly likes. I recount them over and over again. As I tell her a story, I more than relive it, I create it. The translation from unspoken and anonymous into English need not be clumsy; what is sublime is transferable.

MM: Rich's first description was magical: he spoke of dark blue rooms and beautiful men simply wanting to give and be given pleasure. The sense of community and trust necessary for these places to exist particularly struck me. Just knowing where they are seemed like privileged information—and what to do in which place was even more mysterious. He invested in me a new reality with his stories, a new consciousness of a world I might previously have written off as marked by shallow arrogance, or at least dismissed as sleazy and dangerous. Richard brought me partway into this world with the details of his intimate thoughts during intimate encounters, and it is not without cost to him that he has done this. In telling me what it is like on the other side, he now brings my reactions with him when he goes there and must negotiate the physical exclusion of his friend.

RS: When I see the story in Mimi, see her reflecting on it, I suddenly see the magic realism that queer boys pride themselves on creating: the charm and fetish of leather become fetish in every sense of the word. Silent form under blue light: pendulous dicks, sinister slouch, enormous pectorals, asymmetric eyes, ridiculous attitude. But most of all: the man with the eyes of a golden retriever, the one with the strength to lift me on one palm, the man with reptile's skin, or a beak, or wings.

MM: Richard continues his vivid stories, but I cannot go there myself. I am a woman, but I have been mistaken for a man many times since I cut my hair. The first time it happened was in the Atlanta Airport restroom; it was an embarrassment for both me and the "lady" I had to reassure with my high voice. The second time was on a lone stretch of roadway in Orange County where, after about twenty minutes of walking alongside construction traffic, I noticed pickup truck after pickup truck uneventfully pass me by. Where were the horns, the cat whistles, the comments? A bell rang out in my head: they think I am a man. The tension I had been walking with turned momentarily to a gleeful skip before righteous feminist anger set in.

RS: Even in San Francisco, anonymous sex is still a category apart, a closed narrative. Like a privilege, anonymous sex provides the participant with a perspective particular enough to ape a single objectivity. Not knowing names, we name one another: shy bottom, old lech, Skippy, closet case, Bionic Saliva Glands, Straight-Boy Cocksucker, Mr. Blue Saturn. These names cohere from one trip to the next. They reinforce the single narrative. This is why the stories are good. Nine times out of ten, in fact, the stories are a good deal better than the sex.

MM: When I moved to San Francisco, I began to encounter a new form of gender misrecognition. Quite the opposite of the construction workers who now ignored me, men of another ilk give me more attention than I ever got as a long-haired girl. After a few walks along Castro Street, I understood their long looks, taps on the shoulder, and mischievous smiles. They thought I was a man—a gay man. I like this attention, and I share some of the disappointment these men display when we realize I'm not what they thought I was.

My positive response to this attention has less to do with our different positions in the history of male domination and more to do with our shared history of secret desire and vulnerability. These men can celebrate the erotics of objectification out in the open. Here I am passing through an environment that is neither hostile to nor disrespectful of women, merely indifferent.

I am excited when I am momentarily included in what I have come to think of as the most male of all spheres. Far more than Congress or a golf course, the gay male world is a place that decides what is and is not "manly." Gay men have the power to claim even the most masculine of signs, a police uniform, for example, and make it queer camp. Power to the Village People. I have several straight male friends who will not wear mustaches without a beard because they think it would be sending out the false message that they are homosexual. And who wants to get mistaken for a gay man if you're not one? Unless, of course, you're me.

Rich took me to the northern section of San Gregorio Beach where naked men of every shape and size prowl along the sand between the water and a series of small fortresses constructed with driftwood and boulders. These semipermanent structures, many quite impressive in architectural design, are rigged to provide some shade and to break the wind coming off the ocean. More important, they offer a degree of privacy to their occupants. Not owned by anyone, they shelter a community of men who ritually stalk one another for the erotic pleasures of sun and sex.

RS: San Gregorio is the sort of place that displaced East Coasters moon over when they reach California. People have sex here because it is a beautiful place. It's never been a place for sex for me: I prefer places that are beautiful because people have sex there. At the beach, the perspective is not fixed: some men come for sex, others are revolted by it, still others are indifferent. Mimi is fascinated. We sit over our picnic as she muses about what I thought might make her uncomfortable. By and large, the men of the beach accept her as male and assume that she knows the language. What she perceives, however, is more an absence of language.

Her questions defamiliarize the environment for me. She wants a system, a tool for understanding what must appear to be bizarre behavior. Why do these men wander back and forth through this little community of half-buildings? They are clearly not going anywhere, nor do they have any apparent goal. They stroll, saunter, stand, and smile. It's a nice day at the beach, but nobody seems to be sitting down. There is enjoyment here and wordless communication. Stared at as perhaps never before, Mimi feels preyed on by creatures more "natural" than herself. Her idea of the natural—that this is some primal mating ground, a habitat of instinct—both attracts and disturbs me.

MM: The repeated pass of men accidentally plying their manly wares in my boyish direction thrills me. Maybe it's because I am realizing for the first time that sex is as natural as the crashing waves. Maybe it's because I feel appreciated in a world where I typically feel superfluous. My thoughts bounce from an appreciation for the pure perfection of our animal nature to the daunting division that still exists between them and myself. I am drawn into this primal mating scene, but when they pass close enough to recognize my femaleness, that is the end. As close as Rich and I have become in this place, I still cannot walk in his footprints as he leaves our fortress to prowl the beach.

Rich saw my fascination with San Gregorio and with his South of Market life, and he began to see his world a bit through my eyes. When I expressed my desire to see more of his male-exclusive world, he began conspiring with me to make this possible. I wanted to see these dark rooms, to exploit just once the potential of all that erotic energy gay men mistakenly sense in me.

RS: Under her three layers of drag clothes, Mimi's tits suddenly read as she moves into cruise mode. Her hips merely read as a big ass (small mercy).

MM: Because I realize I am, in large part, thrill seeking, I feel comfortable only if I do not put a damper on someone else's good time. Rich and I also agree that my experience would be very different if I presented myself as a woman in these places. I want to pass for a man so that I can feel as if I'm a member of this particular community. My stakes as a female-identified queer are different from those of male-identified queers, or female-to-male transsexuals of any sexual orientation. I'd like to have a real penis of my own, just for a day, in hopes of learning something new about living life quite happily without one.

RS: The walk complements the body, and any disharmony, for example, pasting my walk on Mimi's body, will be obvious. I question—to myself—whether Mimi might not walk better in the lingua franca of the straight male—straight on, head cocked back, large chest, large ass—kinetic rather than potential energy. Our bodies are different in instantly readable ways.

MM: There are a few things I need to work on. My voice, probably a natural alto, is a socialized soprano. Rich puts his finger on my neck and tells me to speak so that I can feel the vibration. There is some difference when I'm concentrating, but I have so finely tuned the high pitch of my "don't worry, I'm not threatening to you" voice that I easily slip up. I look at Lou Sullivan's *Information for the Female to Male Cross Dresser and Transsexual* for a few more tips. He stresses relaxation, breathing, intonation—don't say everything like a question, he suggests. I try hard to feel as if I deserve to be speaking, as if people care what I am saying. Still, I feel much more confident the next week when a cold lowers my voice for me.

My breasts are a problem. Because I have grown up slouching to conceal them, sticking my chest out to walk tall and proud makes me feel very vulnerable. Not to mention counterproductive if I want to present a man's flat chest to the world. If I hold my body in a masculine way, the most feminine parts of my body are on display. I do not feel comfortable "binding" them as Sullivan suggests, but two jog bras do seem to help.

RS: I help Mimi practice walking like a queer boy. She actually gets it well enough. As we start to break down this walk I know too well, making it an acting exercise, we find the minute level on which gay men communicate. The slightly asymmetrical swagger. A bowing of the legs and a slanting of the chest. Like the dress on the transvestite, every aspect both masks and indicates a penis. This is going to be complicated.

MM: Most important of all is my mental attitude. I have to look at men and let them look back. I have to own them rather than feel the threat of their owning me. I am the predator, not the prey.

Richard suggests we try an intermediary step first. The Hole in the Wall is usually all men, but women are not explicitly excluded. It's a bar, but sometimes, especially on weekends, men have sex in "the back."

RS: The Hole in the Wall is unique in San Francisco. It both intimidates and draws just about every demographic sector of the city's gay male population. Most people who have never been there think of it as a leather bar. It is not. It is a dive that has largely maintained its identity as a dive, despite waves of club kids and slumming professionals. Dimly lit and familiar, most of us can find a nook. Sex occurs there, albeit less frequently than before.

MM: A number of men of all shapes and sizes stand in the back, some with their arms around each other, some kissing. There is something very lesbian about the way two men kiss when they share affection as well as lust, a joy of engagement without ownership. Lust without honest affection can be very sexy too, but there is a way in which the excitement resembles a successful business deal more than a personal interaction. Your stock rises and falls depending on your ability to read the signs.

RS: We chose this bar for three reasons. Though the dominant strain of customer could be described as biker, Mimi would not be uncomfortable in the drag that masks her best—postcollegiate flannel shirt and jeans jacket. We call Mimi Erin/Aaron.

MM: Kissing aside, nothing I would call "sex" is happening at the Hole in the Wall. We sit on a high bench along the wall near, but not in, "the back." A friendly and extremely wasted man hands us a joint and introduces himself as Barry.

RS: One almost surefire method of indicating her maleness is through our interactions. When I treat her as my boyfriend, adding a dash of top/bottom, she definitely starts to pass. We walk hand in hand, me leading. We attract a great deal of attention. We order beers and sit down. Next to us sits Barry, large, boyishly happy, and about eighteen sheets to the wind. We introduce ourselves, and he seems to accept Mimi as Aaron. He watches us carefully, picking up on the top/bottom dynamic. My hands move wherever they want. Aaron keeps hers to her sides.

MM: Barry watches us, and I sense he is puzzled until Rich puts his hand on my upper thigh. Then Barry grins broadly. "You guys just look so great together!" Triumph. I try to observe other things. In the back of the Hole in the Wall is a wall full of holes:

photos of men's butt holes displayed on the wall. Backsides in the back. Holes on the wall at the Hole in the Wall.

Rich tells me it is rumored there is one woman up there. The temptation to go over and find her is very, very small.

RS: A fortyish man in a sweater and glasses informs Barry that Mimi is a dyke. Barry's confusion knows no bounds. One of the things that probably made Mimi believable to Barry was the fact of our top/bottom signals: women, dykes in particular, do not generally allow themselves to be touched as freely as queer boys touch each other. They do not give back rubs to men in bars when told to. Other men try to come to a decision about Mimi's gender. A leather dyke couple across from us, it should be noted, is uninterested. Someone says Mimi looks like the lead singer of the Smashing Pumpkins—then pauses for her reaction—"but he's a guy."

MM: On another night, I meet Rich at the Jackhammer, a Castro leather bar, where he works. It's "the workingman's bar," but I feel more out of place for wearing a blue work shirt without leather than for being female. It's a quiet night here, and all I can do is imagine what goes on during the "yellow hanky beer busts" on Wednesdays. There is a Tom of Finland drawing on one wall and a poster of Mr. Leather 1990–something. Strange high wooden structures resembling benches stand empty in the middle of the room. I picture scantily leather-clad men on them in a variety of acrobatic positions engaging in exotic behaviors. When I ask Rich what they're for, I'm ready to believe anything. "People sit on them," he says.

Finally Richard and I decide I'm ready for the final step into the world of men most closed off from me. I will go with him to places where there is always sex going on; I will see men together, and I will feel their looks on me. I will be a part of Richard's other world, a world of men with men for men—a world where women are not relevant to the matter at hand, even as merchandise.

We first try a few bookstores on Folsom Street. The one called Folsom Gulch particularly excites me because I have noticed it before. One late afternoon last fall as Rich and I were riding our bikes home from the train station, he told me he was thinking about whether or not to stop by there for a quick blow job. I remember feeling a combination of envy and amazement as he turned the corner, parked his bike out front and walked in. I continued home, wondering what that kind of sexual availability must be like. Would I even want to do that if I could?

It is not that the occasional lesbian sex club does not exist or that anonymous sex with men is not available to any woman who is willing to put herself at their mercy. The question goes far beyond risk or simple availability or even morality. Richard could not do what I am doing with him now. If he were to disguise himself as a woman and go to a lesbian sex club, he and I would have to ignore the dominant dynamics of our world.

RS: Folsom Gulch and its companion across the street are your standard homosexual dirty bookstores. They attract both very out queers and very closeted individuals from nearby downtown places of employment. At the front of the store is a cashier, with racks of magazines and videos conveniently placed for easy cruising. In the back is the true cruise area: twelve video booths ringed by a rectangular corridor. Mimi is to walk in first; once she's safely inside, I'll enter as well. It's getting a little "Wild Kingdom."

When I get up to the cashier, I look around and see her in the back, staring at a *Honcho* magazine with strange intensity. I find out later that the cashier was unexpectedly friendly, thereby throwing her from her purpose.

MM: I felt my femininity following me around like a spotlight from the sex-toy rack to the video shelf. We try again across the street.

RS: I watch her through the window as she buys her tokens and goes in. Inside I find her leaning against a wall. The presence of a woman in there feels completely absurd to me. But no one seems the slightest bit confused about her gender: she is unquestionably male. Her stance has shifted into the quiet slouch pose that most of the other men against the wall hold. Her eyes stare out, just below eye level, ready to meet a glance should someone attractive walk by.

MM: I'm in. I did it. I am in the "back." Men stand along the outer walls looking at the doors of the booths and at one another. And at me. It is much darker back here. What a relief. Some men look at me with interest as I circle the island of three-by-three cubicles. I walk with confidence until I can situate myself in a corner and relax. Reading the signs on the wall, I chuckle at what must be old jokes for the regulars to these places. NO LOITERING!

There are older businessmen, young pierced queers, white, Asian, black, thin, chubby, cute, not so cute, and no one seems to be in a hurry. Where there are not real men leaning against the walls, there are life-sized painted images of men standing in sexually suggestive poses looking back at you. Even the decor is loitering.

RS: What is looked at here is generally more constricted than on the street. The set of glance, the speed of your walk, the size of the crotch, and the placement of the hands all hold a very particular currency. It constricts the movements of the visitors into a limited argot shared by all. It choreographs. It creates a certain tension, a moment. It is this sense that identifies an all-male environment for me. Mimi, though nervous, has fallen into this scheme almost unconsciously.

MM: ONLY ONE CUSTOMER PER BOOTH! Some men make the rounds and try a door every now and then. Others try every door. Doors are locked, unlocked, opened, closed, all in short periods of time. Sometimes a man just opens a door, looks in, and closes it. Other times, they step inside and come out in less than a few seconds. One man goes in, two men come out. One man goes in, another follows. Another comes out. It resembles a *lazzi* in the Italian commedia dell'arte theater. Some of the men leave the arcade when they come out. Others make another circle around the booths, cruising for new prospects along the loitering walls.

Here everyone is not only allowed to have a body, but the overall silence of the place makes the body primary. I am part of this sign language, and it seems as though only Richard and I are aware of the distance I represent in here between signifier and signified. As I relax into the wall, I feel the power of my height, my weight, my boyish good looks. I casually rebuff the subtle entreaty of a fifty-year-old white banker.

On some of the doors are signs that read: THE BUDDY BOOTH! PRESS A BUTTON AND WATCH SMOKED GLASS DISAPPEAR TO REVEAL THE OCCUPANT NEXT DOOR! Richard has already described these miracles of modern technology to me. I very much want to try one out but am afraid I will disappoint my "buddy" when he puts his quarters in the slot. I wait for two booths next to each other to empty out and quickly enter, locking the door behind me. My heart is racing.

RS: Mimi and I had agreed beforehand not to appear to know each other while there. We would draw each other's attention to what we found interesting or characteristic by "cruising" each other or simply indicate something by looking at it.

MM: Fortunately, Rich has seen me and has gone into the other one. He taps on the gray glass, and I hear him put his tokens in. I do the same and press the "yes" button. Lo and behold, my reflection in the glass turns into Rich, standing there looking back at me. We burst into stifled giggles and pose for each other for a minute or so. I grimace at the sticky walls and floor. We giggle some more. Then I convince him to come in to my booth with me.

At this point, I am feeling even bolder. I want to watch other men. There is a video screen with two guys fucking each other in some military scenario. A token gives you about two minutes of this. I want real men. We hear someone enter the booth next to us, and quickly we discuss what position we could get into so I could see them without them really seeing me. Rich pretends to give me a hand job and we grind our bodies against each other. As I grab his back, I peer over his shoulder at our "buddy." It is an extremely attractive young black man dressed in white. I'd noticed him before. I guess he'd noticed us too. Rich mutters questions, masked as dirty talk. "What's he doing?"

"He's staring."

"Is he jerking himself off?"

"I can't tell."

"Is he curious or horny?"

"I don't know. He's male."

"Do you want to come?"

"No, I'm not ready yet."

RS: It is her time to savor a bit of the control. This is drag at its finest, perhaps: interactive. She has achieved the phallus, though not a penis.

MM: My eyes meet the man's for a brief moment. He looks desperate. Then the glass goes gray. We have run out of tokens. Rich and I zip up and leave the booth together looking satisfied and head out into the bookstore.

RS: We have our own sex story.

MM: Let's go to My Place, he says. On our way, we talk excitedly about our experience, our intimacy, our impressions. I was not unaroused by our performance, and I feel very close to Rich.

RS: My Place is a step or two beyond Hole in the Wall in the category of outright sleaziness. Sex occurs in the back on a regular basis, especially in the corner adjacent to the toilets where the view from the street entrance is obscured. Painted black throughout, with vivid and graphic murals, the place actually has much more of a standard gay-bar feel to it than the Hole does. Whereas the front half of the bar can be quite friendly and loud, the back tends toward a more visual aspect. Men pose in a scene imaginable to anyone who has seen the film *Cruising.* The night we are there, all the attention fans out from a very involved bout of oral sex engaging about five different men.

MM: When we get there, it feels almost natural to sit next to Rich on a bench made of wooden crates, drink beer, and watch men give each other blow jobs. There is a community feeling at My Place, created through looks, gestures, and a certain spot of honor in front of a giant boot where the horniest men stand waiting for their bulges to be appreciated. Men shift from location to location for a better look, a better cruising angle, or even to speak to a prospect. The sex always seems to involve at least three direct participants: share and share alike. Although I do not go over there, I feel included. I am appreciating these men and their bodies. They see my nods of acceptance and appreciation, and they are glad I am getting a thrill.

RS: One of the most important binaries in talking about sex is that of open and closed. Sex is a world closed off from people in the general sense, a world that includes only those who are participating. But I've come to appreciate bookstores because they are public, open, and therefore safer than the closed environment of a bedroom. Anonymous sex represents a specialized knowledge for me; those who enjoy it have an almost gnostic allegiance to this closed knowledge. Yet the experience is endlessly replicable, open-ended, and transferable.

It therefore means a great deal to me that Mimi can enter this world. My dyke friend in the bookstore was truly an absurd sight. The fact that a dyke could so readily pass means that open and closed have been reversed. The other men accepted her without question, and the more her confidence grew, the more her street value rose. At one point I looked at her and saw the attitude that marks the king of the hill. She looked straight where she chose, without the slightest apparent regard for the judgments or desires of others.

In this case, something was different. It was, "To hell with you if you figure out I'm a dyke. I have a right to be here." I delighted in her deception, but only because I was in on it. The code, the choreography, the experience all are achievable, it seems, to anyone within a very wide set of physical descriptions. The fact that Mimi went through many of the same feelings as any first-time gay man does is also important. In the end, despite all our attempts to tailor her passing to the place, the place tailored her. She could read the cues, and the cues could be read on her female body. My would-be closed narrative endowed her, the most excluded one, with total power to view, act and see with new eyes.

MM: I've never wanted to be a man. I've just always wanted to stand in a room full of open doors rather than closed ones. The first few moments of watching two men have sex at the bookstore filled me with guilty excitement. I was breaching their privacy because they did not know I was there. As they continued, however, the view they gave me became so clear that I realized they did know. My genderless eyes peering through a makeshift peephole were attached to their fantasy too, and it added to all our pleasure. My guilt turned to calm acceptance. I had entered a world previously closed to me, and in that moment all three of us were the same.

When I walked outside to Richard, I felt a kind of relief I had never felt before. I was leaving because I wanted to, not because I had to, and I knew I could go back. What's more, Richard knew, and that was enough for now.

CHAPTER 11

Recognizing the Real: Labor and the Economy of Banjee Desire

Lawrence Chua

I was born in the gut of Blackness
from between my mother's particular thighs
her waters broke upon blue-flowered linoleum
and turned to slush in the Harlem cold
10 P.M. on a full moon's night
my head crested round as a clock
"You were so dark," my mother said
"I thought you were a boy."

—AUDRE LORDE
"To the Poet Who Happens to Be Black and the Black Poet Who Happens to Be a Woman"

In the islands I am tempted to call home, everyone works. Whether that work is assembling microchips in a Penang factory, keeping watch for *los feos* on a Loisaida street, or entertaining pink-faced tourists in Waikiki, labor takes up the best part of our lives. On these black islands under the sun, our skin coloring most accurately resembles the shiny hue of currency.

Our sexuality, like our labor, rightfully belongs to us, but the fruits of both are systematically stripped from us. Just as colonialism, industrialization, and economic "globalization" have changed our relationship to labor and production, they have also changed our ideas about sexuality, gender, and pleasure. At the onset of the Industrial Revolution and the era of imperial conquest, women from a variety of cultural backgrounds who performed menial, paid work were considered "manly," "unsexed," and "a race apart." Children of diaspora and plantation lullabies, we continue to live in a culture that devalues our labor, particularly women's labor, and sees the physical evidence of that labor as unattractive.

Yet so many of the visual cues that we find sexy on a butch dyke—calloused palms, thick arms, truck-driver dress code—derive from those same working-class traditions. In the house balls of Harlem, "banjee realness" has been a basic category for young black fags and dykes to assume the macho finery of the street, copping style and attitude from urban poor and working-class legacies. Just as multinational capitalism has intensified a plantation economy in which the global workforce is primarily black and the ruling classes who profit from their labor are primarily white, butch codes have also become even more distinctly racialized in the last decade. In its most threatening incarnations, banjee realness risks replicating a stereotype of proletarian life to revalorize what has been historically devalued. But is the banjee realness that is so pervasive in black urban and lesbian vernacular culture today a form of class transvestitism or transgression? Are bull daggers and banjee divas merely dicks in drag? Or are they on some other shit?

In the midst of today's rampant commodification of sexuality, hedonistic sexual pleasure has come to serve as a stand-in for radical, liberating, political practice. Instead of a vision that refuses the Cartesian duality of mind and matter, which could free our spirits as well as our bodies, capitalist culture would have us believe that just rendering some of our bodies visible is equivalent to social change. But history has shown that to co-opt any radical culture to the logic of industrial discipline, it has to be rationalized. And to be rationalized, it has to be systematically represented.

Now that black drag queens are being used to pimp cheap makeup, homophobia is finished. Now that we're all plugged into *Yo! MTV Raps,* now that we all buy the same baggy jeans and baseball caps in the same malls, buy the same commercialized forms of black vernacular language, racism is over. We are the same. Marketplace has become an instantiation of community.

From the pages of glossy lifestyle magazines targeted to gays and lesbians, to more widely distributed music videos and movies, the bodies that are most valued in consumerist culture are, surprise, those white, buffed bodies that economic privilege produces. In this context, the bodies of black people—African, Asian, Latino, and Native peoples—are a cheaper form of merchandise. Desire for these bodies is usually framed as a kind of commodity fetishism. A hot back room or beach in their islands is often described as a "supermarket" or a "candy store."

Yet in the midst of this lust to consume, new sexualities are emerging, sexualities that not only defy compulsory heterosexuality but also challenge our ideas of sexuality based on the tired binaries of straight, gay, and in-between bisexual.

One day I woke up with that familiar stiffness in my bones gone. One day I woke up and all the names you gave me washed off my back in the morning shower. What would it be like to dispose of the clarity of gender? To slough off my "gayness" or "bisexuality" like so much sweaty attire? To stop reading and writing about difference as otherness. To stop responding to difference with totalizing sameness.

The frequently voiced fear is that by losing our names, we will also lose the power of agency. But it is that same gender identity that keeps heterosexuality such a coherent fiction. The problem with merely creating descriptions for experiences that have previously gone unarticulated is that the words become a prison. There is little movement once the type has been set.

If gender identity is a propertied state, whose pussy is this? Who made it a sin to commit the act of love without intending to reproduce the plantation's labor force? Activism based on Western metaphysical dualism asserts that without property in the self, there can be no subjecthood and, therefore, no agency. In "Gender" for *A Marxist Dictionary,* Donna Haraway writes: "A concept of a coherent inner self, achieved (cultural) or innate (biological), is a regulatory fiction that is unnecessary—indeed, inhibitory—for feminist projects of producing and affirming complex agency and responsibility." Buddhist philosophy teaches that people are made of multiple, gendered parts that are interdependent with one another as donors and recipients and that maintain the flow of elements through the body and the world. For me, that multiplicity is echoed in the practice of many butch dykes.

To describe banjee realness as merely "female maleness" or "female masculinity" is misleading. What we struggle to name as butch, banjee, bull dagger, or gangsta bitch lies in the dialectic of strength, pleasure, and power. In other words, just because you run the fuck don't make you butch.

In *The Myth of the Black Bulldagger,* Diane A. Bogus underscores the relationship between black labor and sexuality by invoking Sojourner Truth's impassioned query, "Look at my arm! I have ploughed, and planted, and gathered into barns, and no man could head me! And ain't I a woman?" Bogus reminds us that like Truth, the Black Bulldagger "has had to struggle for her place in our minds . . . we have not seen her humanity, nor her loving, and have only begrudged her strength, power, and woman-loving nerve."

In *Stone Butch Blues,* her resonant novel on the making of a butch labor activist, Leslie Feinberg arms her protagonists with their own loving desires, enabling them to emerge as integral components of a far-reaching fiction once called humanity: " 'You and I have to hammer out a definition of butch that doesn't leave me out. I'm sick of hearing butch used to mean sexual aggression or courage. If that's what butch means, what does it mean in reverse for femmes?' "

In the cold comfort of most gay male bars, the fluidity of desire expressed by Feinberg is nearly absent. What does any steroid queen want but a mirrored image of his self-projection? From bar to bar, city to city, the litany is intoned in different ways, but the desire is essentially the same. The model required by gay men in personal ads, drunken conversation, and on-line chats is usually preceded not by the term *butch* but by the words *straight acting,* valuing only the most narrowly patriarchal displays of masculinity. The building of racial and sexual otherness has hinged on that idea of fixity: an identity that does not move.

But it has been a long time since Captain Cook left the legacy of the missionary position in these parts. Banjee sexuality suggests other understandings of the ways our bodies are positioned in bed. Ways that aren't informed by patriarchal power relations. Ways that are far more complex than the words *top* or *bottom* and ultimately deeper than even *butch* and *femme* suggest. Perhaps banjee sexuality is a way to sift through the debris of gender, coming to terms with what turns us on about "maleness" and "femaleness," all the while demanding a critical consciousness of how those roles are used to enforce a division of labor and resources.

If sexual fetishism is the province of "private" domestic space, commodity fetishism inhabits a "public" realm of market space. The division of public and private space, wage labor and domestic work, has been integral to justifying the disempowerment of women and the devaluation of women's labor. You know that line, "butch in the streets, femme in the sheets?" Or perhaps, "looks like a pump, feels like a sneaker?" Why do we always understand such descriptions as a dis? By constantly fucking with our ideas of dominant and submissive, as well as public and private, banjee sexuality disrespects the borders of self and other, wage labor and sexual pleasure.

What does butch desire mean in late capitalism? Is it possible to tongue machismo without tasting patriarchy? The term *fetishism* comes from the eighteenth-century French philosopher Charles de Bosses, who used it as a term for "primitive religion" before Marx used "commodity fetishism" and the idea of primitive magic to describe the modern industrial economy. Later, Freud transferred the term to the realm of sexuality to express erotic "perversions." Western liberal sciences were formed around the construction of the primitive fetish. In *Imperial Leather*, a historical study of gender, race, and imperialism, Anne McClintock notes that "religion (the ordering of time and the transcendent), money (the ordering of the economy), and sexuality (the ordering of the body) were arranged around the social idea of racial fetishism, displacing what the modern imagination could not incorporate onto the invented domain of the primitive." Colonized "fetish worshipers" in Africa, Asia, the Pacific, and the Americas, as well as Europe, were represented as subraces of a white human race. Both kinds of fetishists messed with the linear march of evolutionary progress.

But although fetishism was constructed as a justification for conquest and control, it survived as a form of resistance to conquest. "Fetishism can be an attempt, ambiguous, contradictory and not always successful, to negotiate the boundaries of power in ways that do not yield simple lessons about dominance and submission," argues McClintock. Female fetishism opens up the possibility for new ways of living masculinity as well as a multiplicity of complex desires that do not reaffirm the primacy of the male phallus. Or as radical sex theorist Pat Califia put it, "Once you've gotten two hands up somebody's ass, you aren't likely to feel jealous of a penis."

Economic "development" has disrupted the balance of hunting and gathering, male and female labor roles in the Third World. Pushing tribal peoples in the highlands of Southeast Asia to participate in a capitalist economy has required them to forsake subsistence methods of life. One of the first things they are taught before they are sent into the factories and brothels of the cities is that subsistence is poverty, that material wealth is more important than spiritual wealth. God the father, a white man with a beard, wants you to be rich.

M. Mies wrote about a "feminist concept of labor" that rejects distinctions between socially necessary labor and leisure. In *Patriarchy and Accumulation on a World Scale*, using the model of a mother as worker, Mies shows that a mother's work is both a burden and a major source of joy and self-fulfillment because the goal of such labor is the production of life, not possessions or wealth. Such ideas build on agrarian concepts of work and gender relations. In Thai, for example, the word for "work" is the same as for "celebration." This concept of work developed in rural areas where the division of labor and society was more flexible and egalitarian. Women and men could drop out of relations with their local princes, find and clear new land in the forest, and create new social units. With the work of both women and men valued equally, the sexual division of labor could be characterized by what the Malaysian feminist scholar Wazir Jahan Karim describes in *"Male" and "Female" in Developing Southeast Asia* as "bilateral" relationships: "the need to maintain social relationships through rules of complementarity and similarity rather than hierarchy and opposition, and the need to reduce imbalances in power through mutual responsibility and cooperation rather than oppression and force."

Although such social relationships may sound suspiciously vanilla in the context of sexual pleasure, the idea of mutuality demands that we expose the lie of equality based on totalizing sameness. It demands an interrogation of the dialectic between mere gratification and joy, between an ethic of loving sexuality and base consumer lust. A common description of gender relations among the hill tribes of Southeast Asia is "men without honor and women without repute." Lesbian gender practices can be a way of critiquing such ideas, problematizing the polar categories that sustain compulsory heterosexuality and the oppression of women. Without honor or repute, there's no telling how wicked the loving's going to get.

When white Europeans colonized the Third World, homophobia was part of the program of cultural imperialism imposed on the native peoples. Yet, because of antihomosexual prejudice in Europe, many homosexually inclined men gravitated toward the colonies as a means of escaping discovery at home. Economic "development" in the Third World has intensified the flow of migration from rural areas to large cities that began during the colonial era. Within these rhythms, social meanings are constantly being remade.

I am not suggesting a utopian past to which we can all return, nor am I suggesting that capitalism has been in any way a liberating experience. If farm girls and runaway boys have found a certain freedom and community in urban centers, it's because they have made new cultures through struggle, building on the old through engaging in a dialectic of love and conflict. Just as we have been forced to surrender certain traditional beliefs, black folks have also had to acknowledge the relativism and potentiality of all economic systems of gender, identity, and culture.

The Iranian intellectual Ali Shariarti describes us as "migrants within our own souls." We will always be in motion and never come to rest in one place. We will never live with God. The relationship that sets us in motion—bilateral, dialectical, contradictory—must be acknowledged to understand the complex and interdependent ways that butch sexuality functions beyond inscribing mere identity.

In many black cultures today, the bull dagger and the drag queen are integral to the welfare of those societies. A Hawai'ian *mahu* compared his role in traditional Hawai'ian spiritual practices with the place of fags and dykes in contemporary American society: "On the mainland, the religion doesn't allow a culture of acceptance. Gays have liberated themselves only sexually, but they have not yet learned their place in a spiritual sense."

A 1944 Tahitian–English dictionary defines *mahu* as "to spring up, to grow; cloud, mist, haze; to be satisfied, to quench, to heal; a homosexual; a river in South West Moorea." A stream mediating the body and the mind, butch practices offer up a way to challenge and reimagine black masculinity. Even as it reconnects us to the communities that reared us, banjee sexuality is about making radical incursions into the territories we're not supposed to be in.

When a gay man gets fucked on all fours by a banjee dyke, is it still gay sex? What about a straight man? Does a lesbian phallus taste the same as a gay male one? The world cannot be readily transformed into text or narrative convenience. Desire, like language, is a vibe. Mastering it will never be as rewarding as working it.

Yesterday you and I were sneaking glimpses of each other in the reflective surface of a downtown office building window. You were moving crumbling pieces of lumber on your shoulders. As you stretched your arms, your T-shirt went up above the edge of your waist, revealing the smooth, dark slope of your belly, inscribed with a darker ink that read *E'opu Ali'i.* Sweat twisted across the back of your broad shoulders and arms. I caught my breath and in that instant felt something cooler than electricity surge through me. I wanted to pick you up and throw you through the mirrored wall that separated us. I wanted to stand over you lying in the shattered glass, kick you open, and watch what dreams would flow out. I would wrench your arms behind your back, spread your thick legs and stick my hands inside you, feel the warmth of your insides soaking my skin. I would push my mouth to your face and let the whispers I have been saving over a lifetime dribble down the funnel of your ear. Soak your brain. I am here to fuck up your shit. I am here to tell you how much I love you.

C H A P T E R

Crossing Over

Linnea Due

Shadow Morton works in Stormy Leather's big, airy San Francisco workshop a few doors down from the retail store, fabricating sex toys—wrist and ankle restraints, collars, harnesses, cock rings, blindfolds, gags. Cutting heavy hides, sewing and gluing, punching and hammering demands strength applied in concentrated doses, coupled with a painstaking attention to detail. It's a perfect gig for Shadow, the pierced and tattooed version of wholesome stability with his neat beard, thoughtful analyses of life and love, and careful, shy smile. Shadow Morton used to be a woman. Or did he?

Says a pal who knew Shadow when (no one needs ask when "when" was): "Shadow was on this panel discussion for butch women, and she said that she'd considered changing gender but had decided against it. She said she didn't want dykes to perceive her as a straight man when it was dykes she was attracted to." My friend lifts her eyebrows, then urges, confrontation creeping into her tone, "Ask her that. Ask how come she changed."

We take gender personally, our own and everybody else's. And

Shadow, who now identifies as a gay man, altered not only his gender but also his orientation. Shadow insists he changed neither. He says his real orientation was covered over by his own homophobia. By sleeping with women, he was satisfying what he thought society wanted of him as a man. Now that he's free to be himself—now that he's uncovered himself—he realizes his primary attraction is to men.

Matt Rice doesn't have such a clear explanation for his migration from butch dyke to gay man. The change was entirely unexpected, and it meant breaking up a relationship with a woman Matt describes as "the most wonderful girlfriend in the world." It took a gay male friend to clue Matt in to what he was feeling. "He said, 'Matt, duh, you're gay!' I was floored."

What these men are saying—what these men are living—tells us that gender is infinitely malleable and that we need to question our concept of sexual orientation. Are we oriented to a gendered body, or are our attractions based on that body's sameness or otherness to ourselves? Can this "flip" that so distressed Matt Rice be explained by the truth serum of hormones? Did he, as a transitioning man, become more aware of himself in relation to other men, a growing consciousness that eventually culminated in desire? Or did his orientation alter because of an overriding attachment to queerness, a political and communal alliance strong enough to break what seemed to him unbreakable—his sexual attraction to women? And if that's so, mightn't it be said that Matt is angling for a new position of rigidity in the midst of fluidity?

The only thing different about Matt is that his point of reference is newer than yours or mine. Although we can intellectually accept that much of identity is socially constructed, this doesn't mean we don't cling like limpets to what we think defines us. Far from being a quirky little crowd on the furthest margin of the human stage, transsexuals have come front and center to raise the curtain on what most of us prefer to keep hidden. The human paradox becomes crystal clear: the moment we assume a definition, whether that definition comes from ourselves or from society, doors start slamming shut in front of us, closing off options to who we can be.

There is nothing more defining to our identity than gender. If we're going to start juggling that around, we can be forgiven for assuming the rest of the balls will drop in a predictable manner, toward the earth rather than the sky. If we start out straight, we'll wind up gay, and if we start out gay, we'll turn straight. What could be simpler?

"Try living your life on a day-to-day basis as a gay man who doesn't have a dick," Matt Rice says. He spreads his arms, inviting me to picture the immensity of the problem. He can't escape at his job either: Matt works as a bartender at gay ground zero, the Lone Star Saloon. "Fags feel they have permission to touch you anywhere," he says. "Fags grab my chest, and I'm going, 'Who gave you permission to touch me?' They're like, 'She's so uptight.' "

"The whole she–he thing," I say sympathetically.

Matt nods. "Right. They tell me, 'I call everybody she.' But have you noticed they only use it when they want to insult someone?"

We are huddled around a table on the back patio of Red Dora's, the dyke-run café/arts salon. Inside, against a backdrop of Tribe 8 CDs and posters advertising poetry readings and performances, a bunch of sixtysomething dykes wearing 49er's jackets are eating poached eggs and arguing politics; the twentysomethings staffing the counter smile at them benevolently and dart by every minute or so to top off their coffee.

The sweetness of this scene—like a queer Norman Rockwell painting, late morning light streaming in the front windows, curling the corners of fliers that have hung too long in the sun, the older women with windmilling hands and intense voices, unaware of the fondness of the younger women's gaze—makes me wonder how Matt can bear to leave dykedom for the man-eat-man world of the Lone Star. It seems depressingly allegorical that we've been banished to the dark-as-a-Dutch-landscape patio, in which the steady mist of a February sky occasionally marshals enough energy to splatter us with a few drops of rain. But the real story is more pedestrian: we've relegated ourselves to the backyard because the third member of our party, Jonathan Weiner, wants to smoke.

I've never met Jon before, though I've seen Matt around dyke events since he arrived in San Francisco in 1991. At twenty-six, after two years of hormones, Matt looks bigger, huskier, and more settled in a body that never before seemed to fit him. He was an uneasy woman who often dealt with her awkwardness by letting others take the lead; now it's as if he's heaved a sigh of relief and let himself spread out into the psychic and physical space he craved without knowing it.

Jon, at twenty-four, looks five years younger, and with his crew cut, he seems as if he just stepped off the bus at boot camp. A clown and a rebel, he's the one who'd drive the drill instructor around the bend. Jon recently discovered he loves to dress in drag; he calls what he was doing before—when he was a woman—"reluctant drag." At Red Dora's, the two men bump shoulders, spar together. Jon defers to Matt, who is both calmer and more sarcastic. Matt seems to have taken charge of his life in a way he had not earlier, but his face is as open and mobile as ever.

Four years ago, at an International Mr. Leather contest, Matt bumped into several female-to-male transsexuals, including Shadow. He'd never heard of FTMs, but he immediately understood that these men held a key to the puzzle that was Matt.

"You know how you get one of those moments of clarity? It was seeing them that put that mirror to my face. They were people who could talk about feelings in a language I didn't have. I followed them around the whole weekend like a puppy dog."

Within months Matt had moved to San Francisco, changed his name, and begun attending FTM meetings. "I was still living as a dyke, a dyke called Matt, and I had a girlfriend. I was very male identified, but I was a boy dyke, you know how that exists now? I kept going to the meetings and talking about it for a long time. I needed to be sure I'd made every attempt to live my life the way it was set up. But the longer I was aware of the difference between my body and my identity, the more difficult it became to live my life."

While Matt was wrestling with his identity, other people were wrestling with Matt. "They'd say, 'You don't want to be a man! Eww, yuck, you'll get hair on your back!' I'd say, 'I'm not a man, OK? I'm very male. I am not a man.' When I did make the decision to start hormones, people asked what it meant to me. I said it meant I was going to make my outside match my insides a little better."

"So your body didn't feel right?" I hazard. He certainly seems more at home in this bigger, blunter, paradoxically more graceful Matt. "I'm not a transsexual whose issues are with my genitals," he explains. "It was with my gender role and how I was living in the world, how people perceived me, the way I interacted with people. In a lot of ways, I still feel like a dyke. I didn't feel like a man or that whole sexist bullshit of what a man is supposed to be. My identity as a man is something that's developing very gradually."

"So the stereotype of being a man trapped in a woman's body didn't fit you at all."

"No, it wasn't that clear. I was a little butch girl. I was very eager to please my mother, and I wore dresses when she expected me to. There were no role models for butch women when I grew up. There were gym teachers, so of course that's what I wanted to be."

"Or a Girl Scout," Jon puts in with a smirk.

Matt rolls his eyes. "Jon is such a nelly freak."

"Becoming a man has gotten me more in touch with my feminine side," Jon quips, referring to his foray into drag shows where, he notes dryly, “I don’t have to stuff my bra and I don’t have to tuck.”

“Some might call this is a long trip around the world to come back to the same place,” I observe.

Matt chuckles. “That’s what the guys at the bar say. ‘Why didn’t he just stay a girl?’ ”

“But I’m not a girl, I’m a drag queen,” Jon says, smiling at the guys’ dimness. “I was always a drag queen. Now that it’s not expected of me, it can be fun.” He pauses to light a cigarette with half-soaked matches, an operation that takes three of us. “Being a dyke and then being a gay FTM challenges things,” he says after we reinvent fire. “You don’t have credibility with a lot of people ’cause they’re like, ‘How can you be a dyke and now you’re gay?’ And I’m like, ‘I don’t know. I’m as confused as you are.’ ”

“Thank you,” Matt tells Jon, presumably for acknowledging the confusion he, too, feels. “I remember when I liked nothing better than chasing around the club after cute dykes. But something changed.”

“It must have been a shock,” I say.

“It was.”

“Were you upset?”

“Yeah, ’cause I really loved my girlfriend.” He ponders. “I don’t see women as being any different from me, but women see me as being different. And I have to respect that.” This means he can’t come as close, both physically and emotionally, and it’s clear from Matt’s tone that the lesson has been wrenching. “There’s this whole part of me that’s really involved with taking care of a woman. That's how I was brought up in the dyke community." He had expected lesbians to accept him as he saw himself, as nongendered, fluid Matt. "But why should dykes be different from anyone else?" he asks. There's pain in his shrug.

"Does being a gay man mean sleeping with men?" It seems like a dumb question, but I have to ask. I'd seen Matt back "when" with women, and it was one arena where butch Matt cavorted with both confidence and unadulterated delight.

"Yeah. And you know, I've had so many people say to me, 'I wish you were a real boy, 'cause if you were, I'd marry you in a second.' Finally I said to one guy, 'How would you feel if I said I wished you were white?' What they're saying is that I'd be OK if I'm something I'm not and that I'll never be. So how do I find someone who's evolved enough to not only understand my structural differences but be able to appreciate them?"

The two engage in a spirited discussion of where to find these exalted beings. Jon thinks straight men are the answer: "If they're straight, they won't have a problem with my body—possibly." Even Matt seems to agree: "Straight people are so respectful." But finding true love (or maybe even a date) sounds harder than hard, in other words, scarier and more difficult than it is for any old joe out on the street, who's having trouble enough, thanks, without conflicted gay men (men that Matt has dated are pressured by their pals—"Whatsamatta, can't you find a real man? Are you straight now?"), abusive dykes (upon being introduced to Matt, one woman yanked on his tit and said, "He looks like a she to me"), and the effects of raging hormones (Matt: "Your body is going through puberty and menopause at once, and your brain is on a completely other track where you're traveling a zillion miles an hour trying to adjust to the differences in your social and public and personal interactions.")

All that's before anybody even climbs into bed. "Having sex for me is much more emotionally involved than when I was a dyke," Matt says. "When I was a dyke, I had sex all the time, and it was fun. Now there has to be a much deeper level of intimacy before I can take my clothes off with another person. I need to feel safe and supported for who I am."

He shakes his head. "In a way I'm still gender dysphoric. When people used to look at me, they'd see a woman, and that's not what I felt like on the inside. Now when people see me, they see a guy, but that's not about my past history. When I realized that—" He lifts his hands and makes a silent shriek.

"But isn't it like that for everyone?" my confrontational friend asks. "No one sees anybody's past." Exactly. What it really means is that altering our gender rips away the blinders that hide how little of any of us is ever seen—and how little we see. It's a moment of clarity most of us would rather forget.

How many FTMs become gay or bisexual men? That question was answered in a graphic way at the first FTM Conference of the Americas, held in 1995 in San Francisco, which attracted some 250 FTMs and another hundred interested parties, among them significant others and those considering the change. A board and pushpins were provided along with a map of two axes: from male identified to female identified on the Y axis, from straight to gay on the X. "There was a cluster of pins in the upper left corner," relates David Harrison, creator and star of the much-praised one-man theater piece *FTM*. "Those were the ultramale and ultrahetero. Then the rest of the pins were in this really wonderful blend, all scattered across the board. There were so many gay-identified men at the conference that even we were surprised. I'd say close to half."

The pushpin exercise raises some obvious questions: we assume that people change their physical gender because they identify deep down as the opposite sex, yet many of these men were scattered across the female-identified area. Is this because the change has freed these men to express qualities they'd suppressed before? Did most men know they were gay before the change, or was it a shock? How many had been oriented toward men all along?

James Green, newsletter editor of the Oakland-based *FTM International* and a longtime transgender activist, says no statistics have been gathered to answer these questions, but he's willing to hazard a few observations. "People assume all FTMs come out of the lesbian community. I can't tell you how many people I've met who've had no connection with a gay subculture. Of course, a lot do, but we need to remember that for many people, the lesbian community was not 'the right place' but more like 'the only place.'

"Other people have a real identification with being gay, and what that means to them is being attracted to women. They haven't thought beyond that.

"Furthermore, these are people who have fought very hard to be who they are and where they are. They've struggled to break down barriers, so they don't want to limit themselves with definitions—or anyone else either. Some guys won't define themselves as anything other than 'man.' That's what they've fought so hard to be."

Shadow Morton was described to me as a man both angry and eloquent about his summary dismissal from the dyke community. But when I meet him for a quiet Mexican meal, I get the impression that this is an old subject, one he's moved past. After twice as many years on hormones as Matt, he's full of enthusiasm about his life as a gay man. Clean shaven but for a small beard, the thirty-three-year-old Shadow looks exactly what he is—an articulate, thoughtful gay man. "What I was doing in the dyke world was trying to be a straight man," he explains in a careful, measured voice. "I would grow up, find the perfect woman, we'd get married, have 2.5 kids, and live in a house with a white picket fence."

Shadow identified with his brothers as a child and couldn't understand why his mother wanted to dress him in girls' clothes. "I'd chuck the underwear she was giving me and go into my brother's dresser and take two or three of his. I was so headstrong about it that my family quit fighting me about it. They just hoped it was a phase that would pass." He grins. "It didn't."

When he was around twelve, he figured that if he had a woman's body and felt the way he did, it must mean that he was lesbian. That same year, he went to the first gay and lesbian march in his hometown of Sioux Falls, South Dakota. "I scared the snot out of them," he recalls. "They wouldn't touch me with a ten-foot pole."

In 1977, when he was fifteen, he read about a female-to-male transsexual in a magazine. The article got him thinking, along with his dismay about the way his body was changing. "It was going in a different direction that I had no control over. I felt completely betrayed. I shut down and became neither male nor female and functioned that way for a very long time."

His lesbian pals tried to get him to tone down being so male. "There were key differences," Shadow remembers. "I was much more emotionally detached. When I was with guys—and I don't mean sexually, I just mean on a comfort level—I didn't have to explain myself, I didn't have to process things. With women, I was constantly explaining my motives, my words, my actions." He lifts his eyebrows, trying to communicate how exhausting and frustrating this was.

I remind him what he said at the butch women's panel, about not wanting to change gender because he was turned on by dykes. He smiles, not at all defensive.

"Surprises, surprises. I'd been with women for twelve years, and I figured that was where I was supposed to be. But when I started paying attention to what triggered my sexual arousal, I figured out it was gay porn and watching other men's bodies. I thought, 'Maybe it's just 'cause I want that body so that's what I'm attracted to.' "

"Did this start before the hormones?"

"No. Before I started the hormones, I had a very clear-cut idea of where I was going to end up. But once the chemical was in my body, everything around my sexuality changed. I'm happy as a pig as a gay male. I don't have to change my politics, I can still be queer. And I don't have to worry about going out there and trying to fit into heterosexual society. I watch my sister at it, with her husband and her kids, and it doesn't make sense. It's like a totally foreign concept to me."

He begins to tick off how it works for him. "I don't tend to be a monogamous person. I'm not looking for Mr. Right. Tricking is just fine by me. I have to be very open about my process and who I am before we do too much, unless we just keep it oral." He pauses. "I'm still watching my friends die around me. There've been lots of people I've taken care of, and there isn't always time to wrap myself in latex when the person's getting sick. I've been stuck by needles twice helping with injections." He lets out a deep breath. "I get tested on a regular basis, and I'm as safe as I can possibly be." He pauses again. "It's hard getting dates. I think I've learned how to handle rejection in a very creative way."

"You tell him pretty quickly?"

"First date or two. I'll go have coffee and talk before I'll be sexual with him. Get a better feel for who he is. Early on in the hormones, I went with a guy to his place, and as soon as I told him, I didn't know if I was going to live. It's the most violent reaction I've ever seen. He started throwing things, smashing things—"

"Heterosexual panic," I say.

Shadow nods. "When someone says to me, 'If I went to bed with you I'd be straight,' I say, 'Tell you what. We'll go to bed, we'll fuck, and then you tell me whether you've been in bed with a guy or a woman.'" He laughs. "It's a great line. It's worked several times. And there's no argument once we get done. What women have been telling me for years is true: 'You fuck like a guy.' "

Men like Shadow and Matt and Jon are not what the doctors had in mind when the fledgling practice of gender reassignment came into being. "They were invested in taking sissy gay boys and transforming them into straight women," Shadow says, "and taking tomboy women who were socially unacceptable and changing them into straight men. When a few of us started popping up who didn't fit those categories, they freaked."

Lou Sullivan is famous in the FTM community and beyond as a man who knew what he wanted and refused to back down. In the late 1970s, he presented himself to the medical establishment for what he was—a biological female who had been living as a gay male. Over several years, he tried to get treatment but was refused, owing to the prevailing opinion that there was no such thing as a gay transsexual. This shortsightedness likely had roots in the erroneous assumption that transsexuals are homosexuals who can't accept being gay and who therefore must alter their biological sex—ergo, all transsexuals want to be straight, which segued quite nicely with what the doctors wanted anyway.

Sullivan was like a bucket of ice water thrown on that bit of wishful thinking. Naturally he was treated as a misguided anomaly. But he would neither change his tune nor slink quietly away. He wrote letters, made phone calls, brought pressure from other doctors and transsexuals, and in 1986 founded FTM (which later became FTM International), partly as a resource for other men who were held hostage by recalcitrant doctors and partly as an educational and lobbying organization. Finally, years after he began his determined fight with the powers that be, Sullivan was allowed to transition.

In December 1989, the FTM newsletter announced that providers would no longer discriminate against gay FTMs. It must have been a sweet victory for Sullivan, who had tested positive for HIV in 1986. He died of AIDS in March 1991, after handing off the newsletter to James Green.

"We can credit him with raising the medical profession's consciousness of a separation between gender and orientation," Green says. Sullivan's insistence punched holes in closed minds, and his questions challenged the way all transsexuals were treated. In some localities, the situation for transsexuals is changing rapidly, although sign-offs from a therapist are still required for every phase, including hormones.

Until very recently, the rules by which transsexuals had to abide were draconian and downright dangerous—like requiring people to cross-dress for up to two years without the benefit of hormones. Only after this trial by fire was the person allowed to begin taking hormones. After another specified passage of time, an FTM could undergo the "top" surgery, to remove the breasts and reconstruct the chest, and later, if he could afford it, he could whip out a cool $100,000 for the "bottom" surgery, in which a penis and testes are fabricated—or substantially less for a procedure in which the clitoris is freed and the labia formed into testes. During or after the surgeries, the patient was encouraged to move to a different area, take on a new name, and not associate with other transsexuals. A successful transition meant being able to pass, even with one's wife.

It's easy to see how this script would appeal to heterosexual doctors and how repellant it would be to queers who teethed on Stonewall. Being in the closet is being in the closet, and besides, not everyone wanted to take the same path. At a February FTM meeting, Alice Webb, a longtime gender psychotherapist and one of the gatekeepers who establishes guidelines for who receives care and on what time schedule treatment is parceled out, tried to convince a somewhat skeptical crowd that the medical establishment really was hearing what transgendered people had been trying to tell them for years: that all this is a lot more complicated than anybody wants to believe and that it would benefit both parties if doctors would work in partnership rather than as Orwellian social police. Webb stated that the prime aim of the medical community now was to bring people to where they felt comfortable. If that meant hormones and no surgery, fine; if it meant surgery and no hormones, sure; if only the top and not the bottom, great. This would have been heresy even five years ago, and to many doctors still, it means stranding people in a freakish no-man's-land, so to speak.

But with the opening up of options—and with telling the truth—come other questions. Who chooses such a difficult path?

A friend is in the process of making the change. She (she hasn't changed the pronoun yet) and I spend a lot of time talking about our childhoods. "But it was the same for me," I cry, again and again.

"Precisely," she says, and fixes me with insistent eyes. She thinks I'm way deep in denial, thinks I should be plunging that needle into my hip. I talk to other people with childhoods similar to mine. They're not bounding off to Tranny Tuesday at the Tom Waddell Clinic either. Did my friend's discomfort reach a point that she could no longer bear? Or is it that just about any day of the week I'd choose discomfort over change? Coward or not, I can't help but believe most of the denial of who I am comes from others, not from within myself. If I altered my gender, who would I be satisfying?

"I am a transsexual man, and in my opinion that's a different gender from what people commonly think of as a 'man,' " says David Harrison in his soft British accent. We're basking in the bright March sun on a plant-filled patio in the Castro. A couple of squat tiki gods, a few orange- and purple-flowered lantanas, and a passel of succulents masquerade as a tropical paradise.

David is thirty-six, a gentle, sweet man who began taking hormones about two years ago. He beams when he tells me about his recent chest surgery and shows off his pecs with barely concealed glee. "I am a pansexual. I use that word because I don't like the word bisexual, which assumes there are only two genders. But I'll tell you, sexually these days, men turn me on more than women do. In terms of what I fantasize about and look at on the street, I look at men."

David both created and performed in his theater piece *FTM*. "I love acting," David says. "I went to acting school when I was nineteen, and I learned how to play women. It was really bizarre.

Even though I looked feminine, I couldn't link it up. It was very difficult for me."

"What did that mean to you?"

He shakes his head. "It had nothing to do with being transsexual for me." At the same time, David came out as a lesbian. "During the late 1970s, I was into lesbian paganism and doing a lot to accept my body as female. I never disliked my breasts as flesh. What I disliked was that I had no choice in the matter."

"You didn't feel connected to them."

"Yes. I had nice breasts, but they would have looked better on somebody else. We used to joke with the MTFs, maybe we could trade some things."

About ten years ago, David trained for a sex information hotline and met his first transsexuals. He became lovers with two male-to-female transsexuals—"at different times," he hastens to add. "Vicariously, indirectly, I began to deal with some of my gender stuff through being with these two people." He describes the process as opening a big black box that had sat padlocked in an attic for a very long time—opening it for a second and then slamming it shut again. "It was much too scary to even think I could be that way."

During that same period, David was working as a dominatrix—"a very femme top"—a job that became the subject of his first play, *Permission.* "I'd go to these sessions wearing a garter belt, stockings, corset, the whole deal. It was totally acting. And I'd think, 'These guys actually believe I'm a woman.' " He still sounds astonished, as if the shock will never wear off. "Part of me was standing outside thinking, 'This is so absurd and funny and ridiculous.' I liked the sexual energy, but as a woman I never had a boyfriend. I could never get into that. There's something about same-gender relating that has always not only been a major turn-on but in here, up in my head, just makes the most sense to me."

Then one evening David's world turned upside down when he went to see Kate Bornstein's play *Hidden: A Gender,* about Bornstein's experiences as an MTF. Thinking it terrific, he went backstage and introduced himself. It was the start of a four-and-a-half-year relationship. "Kate made it really safe for me to look at my gender. I was so terrified. I have never been so terrified of anything in my life. I would have these dreams, go through these bouts of feeling physically weird in my body. I'd wake up expecting to see a male body, feel a male body.

"Over a period of some months I had between fifty and seventy-five dreams about waking up and having had the surgery and what I would look like. More dreams about the chest stuff than having a penis. This is something a lot of people misunderstand. It's not an intellectual change. I was kicking and screaming and fighting it."

Part of why he fought so hard was that he was worried Kate would no longer be attracted to him. And shoved underneath that was the fear that he would no longer be attracted to Kate.

"That it wouldn't be homoerotic? That you would change?"

He nods. "That I would be attracted to men."

"Though your sexual orientation had always been toward women."

"Yes. And for me it was a shattering of illusions. When we met each other, it was like, thank god, where have you been all my life? Here was this relationship I always wanted, and then we both changed. It's like, now what?"

I asked the unflappable Shadow if he thought the soul was gendered. He considered the question in his measured way, took a sip of his 7–Up, and said, "I don't like the idea of a gender continuum because it's so linear. I see more a sphere from which you can take cross sections, slicing them horizontally, diagonally, or whatever. You'd find something different all along the way."

He shakes his head. "The human race is so caught up in categorizing itself, into putting everyone in little boxes that keep everything separate. But so many people are coming together and blending, whether about gender or race or culture, that those boxes no longer apply. And people are freaking out because there's no longer a nice set order to how things are supposed to be."

I picture Shadow, over coffee, delivering the news to a prospective date. How he must hate it! And I remember an evening when a butch fuck buddy told me over dinner that she was moving in with a lover she'd never mentioned during the two years I'd known her. "But why have you never talked about her?" I asked.

"It's not a her, it's a him," she said, her face practically in her plate. I was speechless. And while I sat there paralyzed, I was desperately thinking, I've got to say something, she's drowning, but for far too long I could not. Such are the certainties of the assumptions we live by and the sick free fall when those assumptions crash into hard reality.

Transsexuals live in the real world of fluidity that almost no one else wants to see. Who cares to remember that who we think we are might not have all that much to do with us, yet it governs almost everything we do? It's like being the one sober person in a roomful of drunks. There's a certain satisfaction in staying sentient, but it can also be damn lonely.

CHAPTER 

If Two Men Are Having Lesbian Sex Together . . .

Roberto Bedoya, Robert Reid-Pharr, and Eric Rofes

As leather men from throughout the nation converged on Washington, D.C., in January 1997 for the annual Mid-Atlantic Leather Weekend, three gay men met in a hotel room to engage in an informal conversation about lesbian sex. One of us (Roberto Bedoya) had never met the other two (Robert Reid-Pharr and Eric Rofes), and those two knew each other only slightly. For more than three hours we talked about our friendships with dykes, our feelings and fantasies about lesbian sex, and what we've learned from lesbian sex cultures over the years. This is an edited transcription of the talk.

Robert Reid-Pharr: When Eric first asked me if I'd have this conversation, I told him that I didn't know anything about lesbian sex. He said to me, But you've actually written about lesbian sexuality. And I was like, I did? I think and write a lot about lesbians as part of the political movement, about feminism, about lesbian writing. But I haven't really thought very much about lesbian sexuality, largely because I generally don't think about females in terms of sexuality.

Most of the conversations that I have with men about sexuality and about sex are about men. I never had a real heterosexual existence before being a gay person, so most of my understanding of women's sexuality has come from representations of it.

Roberto Bedoya: I started thinking about this when Sara [Miles] asked me to select images of lesbian sex created by gay male artists and of gay male sex created by lesbian artists for this book. In my research—I was looking at paintings and photographs, not film or video—I was able to find images of fag sex made by lesbians, but I couldn't find any images of lesbians' sexual activities made by men.

I was compelled by this absence. Why was this the case? Talking with people I found, speaking generally, that gay men don't have a problem with women's psyches, just with women's bodies; for dykes a man's body isn't the problem, it's the man's psyche—the authority of a male in a patriarchal society. I mean, I am a fag, I'm a man, and the world is set up around me, whether I feel comfortable with that or not.

My friendships with dykes, with women in general, are very important to me. But in terms of my sexual imagination, images of a woman's body don't really come into it.

The relationship between imagination and friendship is so mercurial. My lesbian friends don't talk to me about their sex, except for comments like "It was hot," and I don't ask them for play-by-play reports. But even so, these friendships have helped me deal with my own sexual desires, my own fagness, my gayness.

I first started dating women and had the hardest time. You know, being macho-culture raised, I was supposed to just get married and have kids. . . . When I met dykes, it sort of made me feel more comfortable with my own sexuality. Dykes were the chaperons to my coming out.

Eric Rofes: For me, too, my history of being gay has been a lot about being around lesbians. When I first came out, I found it much easier to make friends with dykes than with gay men. I remember realizing at one point that all my friends were women—lesbians and straight women—and that I really hungered for gay male friends.

My intellectual understanding of lesbian sexuality comes from being in cogender discussion groups like my current queer study group, or the *Gay Community News* collective in the 1970s and early 1980s. *GCN* is where I first saw women and men argue sex, talk sex—usually argue sex. It was mind blowing to me in my early twenties to have these discussions and see, for example, how abortion was related to my right to sex with men. Or we'd talk about all the gay male ads in the paper, these pictures of men without shirts or with their dicks hanging out, and I'd have to deal with the 1970s feminist analysis of exploitation and objectification and hear all these different lesbian points of view about men's sex and have big debates over things like whether advertisers could use a picture of a woman's nude breasts and so on.

I went through different layers when I started looking at the relationship of women to my own sexuality. The first realization had to do with how female bodies and gender roles play out, in this shockingly heteronormative way, in my sex with men. When I put my hand on a boyfriend's butt, it calls up not a gay image or a lesbian image but a heterosexual image of a man putting his big, hairy paw on a woman's butt. That's hot for me. I might have a strong "ick factor" and be repulsed by many aspects of the female body, but then I might use words like *pussy* or *cunt* during sex with a man.

In terms of specifically lesbian influences on my sexuality, things started to connect for me a few years ago, as lesbian-feminism was shifting into a kind of dyke queer culture. There was a more sexualized lesbian scene, particularly around not the old butch-femme but the new butch-femme, and I found it really hot. It was one of the first times I saw two women interacting erotically and got somewhat turned on. I wasn't hot for the women, but I was turned on by the energy around them, and I started bringing some of the butch–femme dynamic I saw younger dykes playing with into my own dealings with guys.

Robert: I think a lot of men have sex with other men and imagine themselves as female, or they use a vocabulary that places at least one man or one part of a man's body as female. I don't know how often that's true for men who think of themselves as gay, but for men who think of themselves as straight and have sex with another man, it seems more true.

But about what you were just discussing, I don't think it's the case that gay men, or men who have sex with men, have absolutely dismissed the idea that there's a lesbian on their bed stand. I think that the way that "lesbian" has been used is usually pejorative, though, so that if two men are having "lesbian sex" with each other, the notion is that they're not having good sex with each other. If two men are having lesbian sex with each other, the notion is that there's no penetration going on. Two men are having lesbian sex with each other, the notion is that it's some sort of vanilla sex. These are the images men have of lesbians, because the idea of lesbian sex that comes to us from straight porn is that there is no such thing as lesbian sex. There's female foreplay and then the sex happens when the man comes into the room. When the man comes into the room, there's gonna be fucking and before the fucking, nothing is going on. I think part of the difficulty is getting beyond the idea that there's nothing lesbians could possibly be doing in bed because there's no possible fucking going on.

Roberto: There's no penis—and fucking is defined by having a penis.

Robert: What I see in the new lesbian pornography, in experimental video, is a lot of dildos. I've started to see representations of lesbian sexuality that simulate activities I think are hot. I've seen a couple of things in which there are lesbians strapping on dildos and fucking men—sometimes men who are identified as gay men. There's a way in which the dildo is the thing that keeps most of the people from turning into heterosexuals. I don't know exactly how it works, but the point is that the lesbian fucking with a dildo keeps her a lesbian, the man's being fucked keeps him as a gay man, even though it's a man and a woman who're having sex with each other.

But in general, when they think about lesbian sex, lots of men don't think about anything . . . they think about sort of a Swedish massage.

Roberto: It's seen as softer, not aggressive.

Robert: Well softer, less aggressive. I think that's issue number one: fucking is not necessarily an aggressive activity. But when there's no real "penetration" that's going on and there's no ejaculation, any of these things that actually say sex to men, there can't be any sex going on. But the new wave lesbian videos show fucking, and there are a couple of female ejaculation videos out.

Roberto: Oh really?

Robert: Yeah! Haven't you seen them?

Roberto: No. I don't watch or look at much porn.

Robert: One of the things that's going on in this new work is not lesbians saying they do the same things that men do but lesbians showing that the range of what actually happens in women's sexuality is much broader than anything that has been represented, even stuff that's been represented in pornography. You know, all the stroking and the hair combing and the Swedish massage is basically something that comes from frustrated porn. The idea that lesbian sex is at all messy, that there's even fluid, that there's any difficulty in it, that there's any pain involved, that there are any body excretions involved, is something that's fairly new to me.

Of course, I know that intellectually, but it's not something I've seen very much of, you know? I still haven't seen any representation of the blood in women's sexuality or in lesbian sex, the menstruating and those things. The truth of the matter is that if you're not having sex with women, where do you actually see such things? How could you think that's "icky" if you can't ever actually see the representation of a woman bleeding or peeing or shitting . . . anything that happens with women's bodies? I mean there's this nasty body, and the body gets cleaned up by the time it's shown, and then we get to see it engaging in something that's supposed to be like "lesbian sex."

Eric: You reminded me of something I had long forgotten. I was once talking to two gay men I'd known for a long time, who were a long-term couple, and I finally had the nerve to ask them about sex in their relationship, because—like many gay men—I had a hard time keeping sex alive in my relationships after the first two years. They hemmed and hawed, and finally one of them said, "Oh, we're like two old lesbians, we haven't done it for years." I think that the primary way many gay men see lesbian sexuality is that it doesn't happen, that it's romantic, that lesbians live in romanticized units that lack an erotic component.

Robert: In the last six months, I've actually heard a number of very, very progressive gay men who have a lot of lesbian friends and who very much love a variety of women, particularly lesbian women, make the joke, "Golly I would like to be a lesbian." You know, lesbians get so much done in a day—[laughter]—they can build anything, they can cook anything, they can fix a car, they are so capable. I see this idea of lesbianism as having very little to do with sexuality or actual sexual desire, but having to do with a certain type of independent women's lifestyle. So the reason that these men were saying, "Hey, I wish I were a lesbian" is not because they want to have the hot sex lesbians have—right?—but because they want to do things that are not even necessarily associated with lesbian sexuality.

Eric: What're you thinking about, Roberto?

Roberto: I was just going back to the fact that I don't actually think much about lesbian sex. I just don't find myself thinking about it, but then again, I'm kind of weird. Weird or odd or different in the sense that in the 1970s, when I was in my twenties, it was about being a Chicano, doing organizing work for the Farmworkers' Union, being a part of Latino activists' work. I grew up in the Bay Area and I was there when the Castro came into being, but I didn't become active in that world, maybe because it was too white, or maybe because of my age, my own homophobia. In those days, it was hard to be a Chicano fag.

Thank god for Patti Smith, the punk scene, where "outside is the side I take" became a community. That was fun. That's when my sexual identity first took on a more activist role. Then AIDS demanded that my sexual identity be out there as part of ACT-UP. Calling myself queer was also a way for me to claim a complex identity.

Robert: You know I almost never call myself a queer. It's one of my pet peeves, and one of the reasons I don't is because I don't think there's anything particularly 'queer' about my sexuality. I'm rather typical of gay men in that I'm socialized to a well-developed community in this country. My sexual activity is straight down the line what it's supposed to be if you're going to be a gay man.

I think the notion of "queer" implies a connection between what happens when I'm having sex with a man and what happens with a female friend of mine who's having sex with a woman—her lover, or a trick, or what have you. Other than the fact that America doesn't like either of us, how much is actually going on that really connects the two of us in terms of our actual practice in the bedroom? Now there may be a lot that connects us in terms of our political practice, in terms of where we live and who our friends are, but I'm not sure how much overlap there actually is between what's going on in our sex.

Roberto: How old are you, Robert?

Robert: Thirty-one.

Roberto: See, I'm forty-five, and I remember going to see the Cockettes while in high school and seeing them in their genderfuck drag play, which was wild. I've got bathhouse memories,

memories of reading *Tales of the City* in the daily newspaper and seeing myself in those stories. All the pre-AIDS sexual world of San Francisco that shaped my sense of gay is different from the world today's thirty-year-olds have and how they have come to understand the gay community. The generational differences are significant.

Eric: I was going to ask each of you what role the lesbian sex wars of the late 1970s and 1980s played in your understanding of lesbian sexuality. That was the moment when I first started to hear what my lesbian friends were into—which dykes were into S/M, which were into butch-femme—who played in what ways. Before that, there was a lot of lesbian–feminist discourse that focused on serial monogamy, highly romanticized relationships, and nonpenetrative sex. This gave me the impression that lesbian sex was spiritual and beautiful, but it wasn't dirty and sexy. It wasn't hot or energized. There weren't the fluids.

Thanks to the sex wars, sex for lesbians became an event, and a real debate occurred. But even though sex practices between men were contested, gay sex wasn't an event. We didn't critique it, analyze it, debate questions of power, issues of danger, or the broader politics of men's sexuality. We didn't have conferences, write books, or form local organizations about gay sex.

It was through lesbian sex debates that I started to feel a connection with lesbian sex in a way, and then I started to read the material products that came out of it—publications like *On Our Backs* and *Bad Attitude,* and lesbian S/M culture. It was nice reading about lesbian sex and getting turned on to it—and finding out from reading Pat Califia or stories in *Bad Attitude* that what turned me on was about power and S/M, not the body, not who's doing it, but the power.

Robert: I see this differently. In the 1980s, we'd see lesbians and women generally debating the act of sex and what is and isn't appropriate in an act of sex. We'd be looking at what is actually going on between women when they're having sex, particularly as it relates to sadomasochism. I think that it's important to remember that at the same time, what was happening to gay men was AIDS. I don't think it's true that in the 1980s you didn't have a debate or a widespread national conversation about gay male sexuality. I think, however, that a lot of that debate actually got backed up to a debate about health.

At that time, I knew it to be the case that gay men and boys were ultimately coming out into a world in which there was a play of sexual danger—but there also was actual sexual danger. In response, people were making decisions about their safety that they specifically gave the label *lesbian* to—I knew a good number of men who said that they were going to engage in "lesbian sex," meaning that they weren't going to fuck. There were tons of men my age who decided that they were never going to fuck or be fucked. There are plenty of men still making these decisions.

Eric: They used the term *lesbian?*

Robert: Yeah, they actually said *lesbian.* And the whole question about what it is that's possible to do in sex and what it is that we're actually doing when we're having sex became obsessive for a lot of gay men. A lot of what was being said from official channels, especially in the beginning of the epidemic, was basically that all forms of gay male sexuality beyond frottage and kissing were dangerous. There was an immense amount of fear attached to men's sexuality, both for people who were just coming out and for people in the first group who actually started to die from the disease.

So you know you've got a sort of switch, when you had lesbians saying, hey, it's OK to be involved in S/M, it's OK to strap on a dildo, it's OK to hit somebody with a whip, it's OK to be hit. It's OK to enact an entire range of sexual practices that very well may be seen as outlaw practice. At the same time, you have this sort of disavowal by men of the things that were seen as gay male outlaw practices. Bathhouses became this horrible thing that you could no longer brag about: You couldn't talk about that experience because it had to be hush-hush. The government was against it. Many gay people, including gay men, were against it. Certain types of S/M practices became very suspect. Poppers went from being a hugely disseminated phenomenon to being basically absent in many locations.

The questions of do you fuck or do you not fuck, do you suck or do you not suck, do you get sucked, do you get fucked, became real questions that people had to intellectualize beyond the limits of "this feels good to me, I like that feeling, I don't like this feeling." It became a question of who do I think I am, and what do I think my role in the world is, and what do I think my future is going to look like, based on this particular practice.

That's all by way of saying that one of the great differences for me (though it might be specious and not correct) is that I assume that gay men always have to be vigilant about HIV, whereas lesbians in the act of sex have something different going on in terms of health. I mean I know that lesbians contract HIV every day. I know that lesbians die of AIDS. But I don't know that it's sitting on everybody's shoulder in the same way in lesbian communities.

Roberto: I want to go autobiographical for a moment. I remember living in a household with my dyke roommate in San Francisco in the late 1970s and early 1980s, a feminist and political activist who worked with a Puerto Rican liberation group. First of all, she came out as a lesbian to other feminists in this group, so they had to deal with that. Then she got into S/M and they had to deal with that and with that heated debate about feminism, S/M sex, and pornography.

I was living in the household not because of my sexual activism but because of political activism concerning race issues. I was in my own kind of Latino mambo organizing along those avenues, and the other people in my household were in the Puerto Rican independence movement.

But I have these memories of going with my roommate to the pet supply store and helping her pick out a collar, because there weren't leather stores yet. S/M hadn't yet been fetishized so much that there were markets for it, so there was a nice danger—fun danger—thing going on. We'd go and pick out these things, and she'd say, Roberto, what do you think? Her girlfriend was totally into it. Her girlfriend was bi—at that moment in time, it was a mixed S/M community.

Just down at the end of my block, Good Vibrations was open, and there was Susie Bright hanging out at the shop, you know, and I'd go out in the morning and get my coffee and run into her, have our talk. I was mesmerized by dildos—mesmerized because, in those days, I was strictly a top. Getting fucked wasn't something I enjoyed, yet dildos were made less mysterious and clandestine to me by the women working at Good Vibrations. Lesbian sexual ease gave me comfort and knowledge about this world of sexual toys.

Robert: Your description of a culture in San Francisco at that particular historical moment made me think about pre-AIDS questions about a sexual analysis and gender differences among gay men and lesbians. What we're calling the lesbian sex wars were really feminist sex debates, and they were a decade-long event. I think they became an event because they weren't just about lesbians, they were broader. And the women's movement at that point was at a place of tremendous cultural visibility.

Gay men's discussions about sex in the pre-AIDS period were limited, very limited, and they did not become events. For example, there were certainly the NAMBLA debates, but those were confined to a very narrow section of gay men who saw themselves as political sex activists. There was the race debate about black men who sleep with white men and around cross-racial relations, but that occurred heavily in Black and White Men Together and didn't become an overarching gay male cultural question. And the third pre-AIDS issue had to do with anonymous sex, and it usually would come up around sex in parks when the police would raid parks or bust people, just as the gay community was becoming politically mainstream. At that time, you had to decide whether your gay liaison in the mayor's office or the openly gay city councillor was supposed to defend men who had sex in parks. But even that didn't become an event.

I don't think most gay men explored an analysis of power the way that lesbians did and do. Even with AIDS, even with all the terror that came out of the epidemic in the mid-1980s, and even with the shaming of certain sexual practices that went on through AIDS discourse, there wasn't an explanation or a debate to the same extent.

I don't know if this is true, but I imagine that when lesbians fetishize something, they think about it a lot and have lots of feelings about it and analyses of it—body parts, types of people, specific acts. I don't think gay men, for the most part, except for particular populations of gay men, have that culturally placed on us in the same way.

One of the reasons that I find lesbians so interesting is that I can have an intellectual connection with them about issues of sexuality that I cannot have with some, or many, gay males. At the same time, you're still just talking about a tiny community of people who actually are that self-conscious. Since the lesbian community has been so connected to a feminist community, there's been more of a tendency for lesbians to be self-conscious about power relations as women and as differently marked bodies. But it still tends to be limited—not only by class and race and sexual practice and so forth, but by whether you live in San Francisco or New York or whether you live in North Carolina. Those are vastly different places.

So I am as fast as almost anyone you know to attack gay male culture, which basically gets on my nerves, but at the same time I'm always reticent to say that there's this other, better lesbian culture out there.

Roberto: When you actually don't interact with other people who are artists or writers or involved in the movement or working in this or that agency, and you just do your day-to-day going to the bars and your day-to-day living in a certain neighborhood, it's not necessarily the case that the majority of lesbians, certainly not the majority of gay men that you'll come in contact with, will have any advanced understanding of power and how that power plays out on the street, much less in their bedroom.

Robert: In the last couple of years, we've seen the mainstreaming of lesbian culture, with the *Newsweek* lesbian and the *Time* lesbian and the this lesbian and that lesbian. I think a lot of it is wishful thinking on the part of the media, but I also think that there are a lot of mainstream lesbians out there. I can name at least a handful of Wall Street dykes who have horrible race politics, who have horrendous class politics, and who are indeed doing some version of butch-femme, top-bottom but would never be able to articulate what they're doing and have no more understanding of Audre Lorde and Cherrie Moraga than I do.

I think it's important to remember that the worst thing about the gay and lesbian community is that the adage "we are everywhere, we are your brothers, mothers, sisters, doctors, lawyers, blah-blah-blah" is unfortunately true. That also means a lot of very fucked-up baggage is carried into the community.

Roberto: That's true. And the mainstreaming of gay culture bothers me. Maybe it's because I grew up in the Bay Area, but there's a sexual outlaw kind of ethic that I hold on to and try to situate myself in. It may take me to the S/M world, it may take me to lingerie. But I kind of resist normality.

That makes me think of something we haven't talked about: the fact that there are lots of gay men who act like women. The transgendered and drag queen worlds. I'm curious to find how lesbian sexuality is a part of their imaginations.

Robert: When I was young and coming out, there was a whole emerging discourse about race and gay sexuality that was squelched. . . . But the other thing that I most bemoan was that when I came out in 1982 at seventeen, there was also a weird sort of Boston/San Francisco–based androgyny thing happening. There were a lot of men who were saying that the man pictures you've given me don't actually fit who I am. And that I'm man and woman all at the same time and I want to express my feminine side. . . . This was the time of Patti Smith, David Bowie, and other forces in popular culture.

A lot was going on in the culture at that time. The Faeries were more prominent. There was a lot of this sort of men away together in the woods thing that's significantly waned. One of the things that I think happened, especially with drag or men embracing effeminacy, is that it became either repudiated or commodified—as with Ru Paul—and its radical implications were short-circuited.

So that you could have said, OK, if you're a man who dresses as a woman and you're imagining yourself as a woman at the moment at which you're dressed as a woman because you're saying the dress makes a woman and not some biology, then it is possible for you to be a lesbian if you are at the moment engaging in a sexual act with another person who has been identified as female? And even though the transgender movement is now under way more forcefully, I've largely seen the problematization of transgendered identity coming from persons who were originally female and who are becoming men through clothing and operations and medication, who very often are continuing in the lesbian community or are imagining themselves as gay men and so forth. I haven't seen a lot of persons who began life as males wanting to be very vocal about or make some sort of considered statements about what it means to be in this female body, whether or not that body's a lesbian body. I'm assuming that there are transgendered persons who are female out there in the world who consider such things, but I've never heard anyone say, I used to be a man but now I'm a lesbian, which seems like a simple enough statement.

Eric: You made a point about how commodification short-circuited the radical implications of androgyny at a particular moment. When you first said it, I thought that the androgynous strain in gay culture I experienced from the mid-1970s to the early 1980s was cut short because people don't mix gender any more, but . . .

Roberto: They do.

Eric: They do, and there certainly is a lot more drag and a lot more commodified gender stuff in the mainstream and queer media than there was even back in the mid-1970s. But what seems to be missing in the new transgender readings I've done is that spirit that used to surround androgyny.

I remember one guy who was in a support group when I had just come out. I was really young, and he'd talk about the "effeminacy movement." I had no idea what this was, but it really, really repulsed me at that moment. He talked about not having gender and how he wanted to create a world where there wasn't gender . . . you know . . . this was a very different time.

Robert: I want to shift a little bit here and go back to aspects of imagination and sexual practices and the function of the fetishized object. The fetishized object, which may have a gender attached to it, becomes an important part of sexual practices. It's interesting: Like what are dyke fetish objects besides drag? You know what I mean?

Eric: I have a dildo story, though I don't know what it means about fetishized objects. There was a period before AIDS when lesbians were getting into dildos, but they weren't into ones shaped like penises. These were different: a dolphin or fish, other kinds of nature-oriented things. I tricked with a guy once who had a dolphin dildo next to his bed. He had gotten it at a lesbian sex store, and he thought it was much hotter than a regular dildo. . . . I could not imagine. I just remember thinking, "You want a dick. It's gotta be a dick." But he was into shoving this dolphin dildo up his butt.

Anyway, your question gets to the basic point that I wanted us to talk about together: What do lesbians' experiences of sexuality, desire, and identity offer to gay men? What do gay men take away from it? Many would say nothing. What *could* men take away from it?

The most sophisticated discussions I can think of on the topic happened early in the AIDS epidemic, when gay men were starting to understand sexuality and risk and danger in ways lesbians said they'd understood and dealt with for a long time. A bridge was built in the early AIDS movement, based on lesbians supporting gay men dying of AIDS and teaching gay men that sexuality can still be enjoyed even when you realize the profound lethal dangers associated with it. But I haven't heard men talking about taking away much else.

Male sexuality in general, including gay male sexuality, is right in lesbians' faces all the time, and so lesbians have stuff to fight, stuff to take away, stuff they have to think about. But for a lot of men, lesbian sexuality, and women's sexuality in general, is just not in their face.

Robert: We're in the District of Columbia. The District is basically one of the more gay-friendly cities in the country. The center of the northwest portion of the District, which is the most monied and active part of the city, is where the gays are, and they have tons of businesses, especially bars, that are specifically marked as gay and male. I cannot think of a single business there that's lesbian identified. I know places that lesbians own, but not a single business is marked as lesbian.

Now what that means to me is that in my day-to-day interactions, I see lots of images of gay male sexuality. I do not see any images of lesbian sex. I don't even have the option of saying, you know, I'm so sick of those goddamn lesbians, I don't want to see any more cunnilingus, I don't want to see any more breasts.

Eric: Do you have women at Gay Pride in Washington without their tops on? Probably not in Washington. . . .

Robert: It's not so prevalent but yes, there are women who take their tops off. It happens exactly once a year. Women are allowed to take their tops off in a very specific, very contained situation once a year in certain cities in the country and certain blocks in those cities. . . .

Roberto: . . . And certain hours of that day . . .

Robert: And certain hours of that day. They cannot, however, hail a taxi with their tops off. They do not get home with their tops off. They cannot stop in the park with their tops off, you know? If you're walking through a park at twilight, you are never going to meet two women going down on each other.

When I say I don't know anything about lesbian sexuality, it's obviously an overstatement, but part of it is because other than my personal interactions with lesbians and whatever they have chosen to share with me about their own sex and sexuality, there are so few representations of lesbian sexuality around.

Eric: I remember a time in my life when the de-emphasis on sex in lesbian culture was something I admired and even looked at jealously. This was when I didn't feel comfortable at all in my body as a sexually active gay man with desires. I think one of the early appeals for me of lesbian–feminist culture was that it was about politics and values: it wasn't about sex or didn't seem to be about sex.

I've also interviewed and talked to young gay men who say that the gay male community now is so highly sexualized that they long for de-emphasis, for pushing sexuality to the margins of a community instead of seeing it as central. I hear this same talk as almost a whisper behind some of the recent writings—Larry Kramer, Gabriel Rotello, Michelangelo Signorile—that have urged gay men to de-center sex in our cultures.

Robert: I've spent a fair amount of time in lesbian bars, seeing a lot of women pick each other up, and a fair amount of time at lesbian events. I've seen that one of the driving things behind all those events, including the political ones, has been "that girl's cute and that one's not."

I look at lesbian culture, and I always see the sexual underpinnings and the erotic underpinnings and the sexual connections and exchanges that are going on there—even if it's the National Women's Political Caucus or, you know, a mainstream feminist kind of thing. I know who's doing who and what it's about. But I do think that it's positioned very differently in many parts of lesbian culture than it is with men.

Eric: Do you think that positioning sex as they do, they have a livelier kind of space for critical analysis in their community than gay men have?

Robert: My own understanding of being a gay man was that the very minute I came out, not only was there the traditional "being gay is a bad thing" and "you should avoid having gay sex" from the straight world that all of us have to overcome, but suddenly, from the gay community itself, there was also all this "sex is dangerous, sex is dangerous, sex is dangerous."

Roberto: How old are you again?

Robert: Thirty-one.

Eric: How old were you in 1979?

Robert: Fourteen. I really think that there were these weird mixed signals when on the one hand, people were saying, Oh my God, we gay people have to have stop having so much sex, and on the other hand, the grand majority of the gay men that I knew weren't having any sex at all and were very upset about it.

But about your question: I don't know that it's actually true that lesbians have balanced their sexuality in the way you're suggesting.

First, I don't like the idea that there's anything at all virtuous about reining in your sexual activity. Now, if you feel like doing so, you ought to. If you have sexual desires that you decide you're not going to act on for whatever personal reason—because you have a boyfriend, because you don't want to sleep with anyone but him, because you don't want to do the type of sexual activities you're being asked to do, because you're ill, or whatever—that's one thing. But the idea that less sex is better for the community . . .

I am much more interested in the idea that sex is good, sex is positive, and that since there are dangers when people can opt to have as much as sex as they want, they ought to do some sort of risk management in relation to it.

Eric: I don't think anyone here is saying that less sex is better for the community.

Robert: I know, but when people think about what it is gays could learn from lesbians, it's easy to say that lesbians are so much more heady and theoretical and cerebral, and gay men are being led around by their dicks.

I think there's something really wonderful and positive about that side of gay men. And a lot of lesbians I know like this about gay men—they like it a lot. Some lesbians are even trying to replicate that attitude.

I do think both communities could work to figure out how to get past the sometimes fucked-up things that go on in tricking that force it to stay so anonymous. You know what I mean? How can you have sex that doesn't demand you be together with this person for the rest of your life but that doesn't deny the intimacy, the fact that every time you come on or in somebody you are inherently making some sort of lifelong commitment to them.

If somebody's sharing your come, it could conceivably be severely limiting how much life they will have, and your activity with your own come may be saying something about what you think about this person's future. The moment is hot because you know that in coming, even if you're never going to see this person again, all this profound stuff is going on. I mean that's bigger than the coming. It's really a life-and-death type of thing. I think when two women get together and have sex, my assumption is that part of what's hot about it is that there's so much woman hating in our society and women's sexuality is so restricted that in the back of their minds there are always these land mines they've had to dodge in order to reach the point of coming. And that can rev up a whole sexual experience for both partners, even if you're just talking about a trick.

Roberto: I remember my first encounters going out to bars. I was objectified in so many different ways—"you be my Aztec warrior," know what I mean? So I had empathy with dyke feelings of subjugation because of what I'd felt around my racial identity. And in terms of becoming more at ease with my own sexual desires, I've learned a great deal from lesbians about that process. But what can I get from them sexually? How to use my tongue better? How to use my hand better? I don't know.

I have a recollection of seeing *Nitrate Kisses* by Barbara Hammer at the Gay and Lesbian Film Festival in Los Angeles three or four years ago. It was really interesting because here was an audience of around three hundred people, and maybe twenty-five of them were guys. I honestly felt repulsion through the whole movie, but I was trying to be cool because, you know, I'm a guy. Guys are cool.

So anyway, I'm thinking—well, first of all, the women in the film were older lesbians, so there was this weird association, like the way the grotesque is often represented as a woman's body, overweight, kind of bearded lady, all that shit. I'm sitting there and watching this movie, and it was a real test for me.

But it was also about learning. There was all this new information, and at the end I go, oh, now I know something. I have a new knowledge, a visual reference, about how dykes do it. And as I live with that knowledge, my initial feeling of repulsion changes to acceptance.

Eric: Do you think there's some basic distinction between lesbian sexual practices and gay male sexual practices?

Roberto: The distinction of our desire defines our uniqueness. We're all homosexual, but beyond that commonality of desiring to have sex with our own, when it comes to "doing," my body likes the sensations another man can give me. My interest in the charge a lesbian feels around her body is no more than "Good! Go get it!"

Eric: I think the difference between lesbian and gay male sex practices also relates to the default role you expect of each gender, and this is where generational questions come in. One of the things that has shifted and blows my mind is how sex and gender are busting out in ways I never would have expected them to. I've talked to some of my young male students who are heterosexually identified, and their preferred sex act is to get fucked by their girlfriends. I thought at first this must be a very marginalized experience, considered taboo, and maybe it is. But when we had a discussion with a lot of other students, nobody got upset, and lots of people seemed familiar with this possibility.

Roberto: I have had lesbians try to seduce me. I've had lesbians ask me to be a parent—you know, father their kids.

Eric: Including having sex with them?

Roberto: Yes. It really scares the shit out of me.

Robert: The idea of having sex is what scares you, not the fatherhood part, right?

Roberto: Right, not the fatherhood part. But it comes again to personal psychological history. My memories of a woman's body are linked to awkwardness and uncomfortableness. I grew up in a big extended family with many aunts, all very short women with big breasts, who would hug me as a child to the point where I felt I was suffocating in their flesh. So I have a body memory that says I don't want to go there, there's no pleasure there for me. It's not about hating women—I love my *tias.* They taught me willfulness, and their fierceness is an inspirational pleasure. But I don't want sex with those bodies.

Robert: So why don't you have sex with women with small breasts?

Eric: I know lots of gay men under thirty-five who say they enjoy sex with lesbians or want to have sex with lesbians or fantasize about it. I could not imagine in a million years having sex with lesbians. Call me rigid or uptight. . . .

Robert: When I was in a long period of not having a boyfriend and I was having all these really positive interactions with women and particularly with lesbians, I wanted to have sex with a lesbian. . . . I specifically wanted to be seduced and slammed down on the kitchen table by some lesbian.

Eric: I worked in queer jobs for around ten years. Then I come back to the university where I'm not identified as queer and sometimes people don't understand quickly that I'm gay, and I found myself being flirted with by women. That was new for me. And I found myself flirting back. And so that's where it started, and then one or two of the flirtations turned into friendships—people I had lunch with or talked with for hours in the library. Then one night I had a dream of having sex with this woman I'd made friends with, a heterosexual woman, and I had a wet dream over it and woke up terrified. I confessed it to my lover the next night. It was just very identity breaking. I felt very split.

I ended up feeling really good about it because I love seeing shifts in my own sexuality, my desires and fantasies—but I still can't imagine fucking a woman. I can't imagine it partly because I haven't had much experience fucking men. And I can't imagine being fucked by a woman, since I have no experience being fucked by a man. And I can't imagine eating out a woman, because the ick factor there is so powerful and the odor and taste are very alive. And I can't deal with women's breasts even to this day.

Robert: Have you never touched a woman's breasts?

Eric: I've had sex with women, when I was in my teens, but since that time I've never touched a woman's naked breasts.

Roberto: Even the closest, closest, closest women that you have known?

Eric: I've never, never touched their breasts. Never. I've never even gotten past the "where do I look" question when I see topless women at the beach. Where do I look?

Robert: What do you mean, where do you look? You look at the most interesting thing in the room.

Roberto: At the breasts.

Robert: The reason I think my fantasies are specifically about lesbian women instead of heterosexual women is because my sense is a lesbian would be more likely to do something like that in the first place . . . clear off the kitchen table and slam me on top of it.

Roberto: I remember having that fantasy with my roommate, who was the bottom in an S/M relationship. Her top would come over to the house, and I'd have fantasies of her taking both of us. For me, it was just about having to take orders from a sexy top woman who was a dominatrix to both men and women.

Robert: It's not even that I'll act on my fantasies, but I like having them, and I've never tried to squelch them. I like the fact that I can have that type of fantasy, and I like the way it makes me see people who are lesbian as sexual. It gets me beyond the idea that top and bottom have to be male and female, or male and female in a certain way.

I think part of why I generally don't want sex with women is because I assume a woman wouldn't like the kind of sex I do, even though my sexual prejudices are fairly vanilla. I realize that that's not necessarily the reality, but at the same time I also think, oh well, no woman would actually proceed in the way that I'm interested in. I don't really want to have oral sex with a woman, but frankly I'm not that great a fan of oral sex with anybody. What I like is the idea of a woman on top, having her way with me. I really like that idea. . . .

My whole relation to lesbian sexuality is necessarily complicated, and a lot of it remains in the realm of fantasy. But it's important to me to try to understand exactly how complex these things are, and why they are, because in many ways I feel just as close to lesbians as to gay men.

Roberto: Vive la difference!

CHAPTER 14

Los Angeles at Night

Susan Stryker

The sky's as dark as it ever gets in Los Angeles at night. His feet are spread apart, ankle restraints fastened around his biker boots and chained to the railing of the redwood deck behind the house in Silverlake I've borrowed for the weekend from a friend. He's leaning forward against the rail on his forearms, hooded, half naked, a big broad-shouldered guy with thick hairy legs but a smooth backside and a clean-shaven head. The black cotton T-shirt advertising some gay leather bar is hiked up around his armpits, so he can expose more target area but shyly cover the fresh scars, still too raw to show, from his mastectomies.

Trees to either side of the deck screen the neighbors' views of us, while the Ice-T tracks booming on the stereo drown out all other noise. I stand there idly puffing one of his cigarettes, holding a heavy flogger loosely in my left hand and watching his body sway absentmindedly in time with the music. I'm wearing serious play clothes—leather pants and black Docs. My shirt's off because the night's warm and I've worked up a sweat; I enjoy feeling the trickle of moisture running between my breasts. I like the pungent smell of me and the sight of him.

Beyond him I can see the fabulous City of Angels spreading out in every direction, enveloping us, creeping up hillsides encrusted with overlit houses, disappearing into the dull orange glow of early summer haze. Downtown office towers peek from behind the silhouetted palm trees and low-rise buildings that punctuate the broken horizon. I pan the city: a police helicopter hovers in the middle distance, the spotlight tracing search patterns on the ground below. He's still so lost in sensation it would be pointless to hit him again right now.

I enjoy these quiet moments in the middle of heavy scenes, when a partner's physical limits offer a contemplative respite from the concentration required for a methodical whipping. My nipples are hard, but I'm turned outward at the moment and don't really want to focus on my own sensation. I feed one nipple a short sharp twist to appease its distracting hunger and feel a jolt of electricity shoot down to my crotch.

Pleasure's never a simple thing. It always makes me stop and think—a habit that eventually gets me in trouble with tricks and lovers. As my hand returns to my breast, I pause to consider a formal question: Is the link I've made so effortlessly between nipple and crotch anything other than the violent installation of a fantasy that organizes sensation for a reproductive economy? These breasts were artificially induced at a point well into my adulthood. They're prosthetic extensions of a will to translate transsexual identifications into interactions with others, generators of material effects that sustain a desired remapping of corporealized space. They have nothing to do with the physiology of milk, birth, crotch. What then is this genital–mammary connection I've made for myself if not a dream of natural womanhood carved upon my unnatural flesh? Is it the fantasy of coerced unity that arouses me, the dream of conquering unruly embodiment with an imaginary idea? Maybe it's hopelessly nostalgic, but I find pleasure in the fact that he and I can cite the forms of those fictively unified political aggregations we call "man" and "woman" even as we work to consign their current configurations to history. I take in the sweeping vistas of the city and tweak my nipple again. Fuck theory.

I return my attention to my trick's flanks and buttocks, visually slicing him into the parts that matter in the moment. I can't help but dwell on the difference between my distant visual enjoyment of the scene and the overwhelming phenomenological intensities that so recently played themselves out across his skin. I have been in his position before, when the point of subjective presence flees inward from the surface with such force that it breaks down and breaks through to another space and time. Remembering such psychic implosions, desiring that sense of release and transformation for myself, trying to open him up and connect with him, I find myself wanting to literalize the experience of breakthrough. I want to cut him and turn a metaphor into something real.

Transsexuals have such emotionally loaded relations with surgical instruments. Triumph and pain, visibility and erasure, self-determination and inscription by others wrestle fitfully along the scalpel's edge. Sometimes it feels so good to take the blade firmly in your own hand.

I retrieve alcohol, latex gloves, and scalpel from the med kit waiting in the wings of the scene and begin carving a new erotogenic zone of shallow incisions along his rib cage. As if the cuts promise some fresh avenue of escape, he returns from his inward mental journey to reencounter the volatile wonder of his own skin. The surface is lumpy, knotted with hardened lymph and discolored by subcutaneous blood. His neurons still fire frantically, relaying wild information about the energy transferred from the supple leather of my whip.

He cries out. I know this sensation too, as the painless pressure of steel slicing through flesh gives way to sting and burn. I douse his wounds with alcohol then flick open a lighter. The spark produces a magic moment of flesh and flames and blood, an abject, sacred conflagration of contraries that lasts a fleeting instant. I smother the burning alcohol quickly and watch him writhe. Fire at night is always a thing of terrible beauty. I wonder if he experiences cutting the way I usually do. Being cut forces me to confront the inescapability of embodiment. It validates my decision to change shape as my means of continuing to live as an embodied subject, forbids me to deny the pain of the body's necessary failures, rewards me with the body's accomplishments. Cutting reminds me that I am always meat first.

He's back now, summoned to full presence by the fire and the knife like some familiar spirit. He laughs raggedly and blows air heavily through his mouth. He sighs and groans, shrugs excess energy off his shoulders, and shakes it from his fingertips before adjusting his stance. He reaches a hand to his side to smear it in blood, then settles back down with forearms flat against the railing as I start the whip swirling again in lazy figure eights. He sticks his fingers through the hood's mouth hole one by one, slowly licking them clean, body still swaying slightly. I time the whip's circuit to the tempo of his movements and the bass line of the music, catching his ass on alternating sides with each down-beat. We haven't spoken, or needed to, for at least an hour. I'm beginning to tire, though, and decide this will be the cool-down set before we quit. I tell him so, then slow-dance the cat languidly across his haunches and let my thoughts drift.

We'd met several months earlier at some inane cocktail reception in a city neither of us called home. He was standing alone, looking out of place in the hotel lobby next to a potted fern, one hand shoved into the pocket of his tweed slacks and the other wrapped around a bourbon and water. He wasn't living as a man yet, but the combination of oxford shirt, tie, and sports coat with his platinum-blond flattop and facial piercings gave him a faggish sort of flair. The way he cross-cut different styles of masculinity somehow communicated the aesthetic sensibility of a gay man rather than a butch dyke, in spite of his female form. That sophistication of presentation, leading the eye against the grain of the visible body to express an immaterial sense of self, is what caught my attention.

I'm drawn to people who do gender with style. I don't much care what their anatomies look like, which pronouns they usually get called or which they prefer, who they tend to fuck, or how they get off. I just love a good show. He was the most provocatively gendered person in the room that evening, a female-bodied faggot who suggested economies of pleasure that existed nowhere else in sight. I felt a very queer sort of attraction for this other transgendered person—a desire making only the most perfunctory gesture toward the homo/hetero binary.

He was surveying the crowd with a look of utter boredom, clearly on the verge of leaving as soon as he finished his drink, when I walked over with a blunt announcement that I liked the way he did his gender. Soon we were deep in conversation about the semiotics of clothing and how to use the kinetic language of bodies to negotiate a public identity. He told me he was a transfag and a bottom, and I described myself as a "male-to-female transsexual lesbian fag hag femme top who likes to cruise FTM leather boys and very butch bottoms." Fifteen minutes later we were in his rented Ford Bronco, looking for a more congenial place to be a couple of gender queers.

We wound up at the only drag bar within driving distance, where we sat in a corner to talk and drink. A relatively good female impersonation show played on the tiny stage, but it failed to hold our attention for long. We began to compare notes on S/M: leather sex, rather than drag, was the subculture in which we had both first approached the issue of transgender identities. We both had discovered that like transsexuality, consensual S/M practice made it impossible to ignore the body: it provided exquisitely intense and intimate bodily experiences that didn't necessarily involve genital sexuality. But it had also helped each of us figure out exactly which parts of embodied subjectivity we could exercise agency over, which we could decide to live with, what we had to change. S/M, we agreed, offered a far better conceptual framework for exploring these life-changing choices than any scientific discourses on transsexuality we'd found. Changing sex is very heavy play.

By the time Patsy Cline handed the mike over to Diana Ross, we'd moved from shop talk to theory and back, flitting giddily from one critical frame of reference to another. We were such intellectual perverts, we never did get around to fucking that night.

A few months later, he came to San Francisco, and we made a date. His appearance had changed now that the testosterone had started kicking in: his voice was deeper, his smell subtly funkier, his body denser. The flattop had been replaced with a buzz cut, and except for the lack of beard on someone his age, he appeared unremarkably male. The incongruously smooth face worked nicely against the severity of his biker cap, leather vest, and motorcycle chaps, giving him a kind of charming vulnerability. I was wearing a short, tight, backless black velour dress that night, with heels so high I had to take his arm to steady myself. I guessed that he might be scared beneath that cocky veneer, and I wanted to offer him the security of a masculine role in relation to my ultrafemme image. There was no way I could know what it felt like for him, transitioning to male, but a wave of empathy, a fierce desire to connect, swept over me as I clung on his arm. I remembered what early transition had been like for me, when the hormones were first coming on like a strong dose of acid. The estrogen coded and recoded reality, sculpted flesh like putty, blurred the contours of intelligible human forms by layering one gender schema on top of another until I appeared as a shimmering moire pattern in the eyes of others. People interacted differently with me, depending on which part of the pattern they saw at any given moment, and then grew confused or hostile when I failed to continue sending the signal they just picked up. The input from the world around me became as capricious as the shape of my own body, as if my entire life were some vast television monitor and somebody else was channel surfing. I begin to think some essential part of myself might fly away into the ether, like a balloon that's slipped its string.

I'd eventually learned to play with that sort of reality hacking as one of the peculiarly compelling effects of MTF embodiment, but I remembered with clarity when it had been a frightening and out-of-control experience. His experience with testosterone was undoubtedly different from mine with estrogen, but part of my pleasure that night, I decided, would be helping this man find the channel changer for himself.

I took him to the Motherlode, a transgender dive in the Tenderloin where most of the women are sex workers earning their surgery money. It's a surprisingly straight-looking space, in spite of the fact that all the women there used to be men and all the men want to fuck women who have dicks: you don't see much that visually contests heteronormativity. But I wanted to go there precisely because we'd be slightly out of synch with the scene and thus harder to slot into identifying categories.

Half of identity is what you put out, and half is how you're read. We were both obviously making statements, yet walking in to the bar together we were damnably difficult to read. Butch–

femme dykes? A drag and her daddy? A couple of straights? We stood out in the Motherlode, inviting interpretation. We could practically feel the gazes swirl around us, trying and failing to gender us. Woman/man, man/woman, woman/woman, man/man—we changed identities, orientations, and pronouns in every set of looks exchanged with others.

I looked hard at him, wondering whether our self-identifications as dyke and fag were going to bend enough for us to connect sexually this time. "Let's cut to the chase, girl," he finally whispered, leaning over to nibble my ear. "I'm a bottom first and a faggot second. What you call yourself has no bearing on what I call myself. All I want is to get fucked. And as far as I'm concerned I've just got three fuckholes instead of two." Grinning, I took his hand. We left the Motherlode for an S/M party South of Market, where I tied him down, beat him up, and took advantage of every orifice he had to offer.

Standing behind him again now on the deck in Silverlake, slapping my cat lazily against his thighs, I find myself replaying that previous time and wanting his cunt again. Desire, like pleasure, is never a simple thing, and like pleasure it makes me stop and think. Is my desire for him just curiosity about an exotic Other? How much am I like the trannie hawks prowling places where women like me sometimes sell our difference to strangers? Or is he the T-Bird, and I'm one of those women for him?

The endless struggle to reclaim transsexual erotics from the uses that nontranssexuals make of us angers me. But I know that sex between transsexuals is different from what happens in the Motherlode. At least neither is using the other to shore up a more normative sense of self. We've both refigured the identifications and partial objects others cobble together in ways that pass as normal. Object choice ceases to have much relevance as a concept here in this new space, because the objects at which desire might take aim have shattered into bits.

For me to enter him like this, MTF fist inside FTM vagina, is for us both to acknowledge the new reality we each locally materialize by our practice. So it's not the partial object of his hole I want but, rather, the excess that erupts there through his transsexual form, the surplus value of the codes that regulate gendered embodiment. His excess mirrors the archaic disarticulations from which "I" myself am fashioned and through which "I" perpetually refashions itself. Maybe this is the transhomonarcissistic wellspring of my desire. Having traversed the territories of perversion and fetish, we have arrived at last at a realm beyond objects, a world of phenomenal flows. The de-territorialized flow itself is what I long to stick my hand in.

I am fisting his cunt hard, striving against the thin membrane of his flesh and the distance of the stars to touch the night sky over Los Angeles. Self crumbles here into the force that structures it, glittering shards of memory shedding like viruses into the blackness. I'm lifting him off his feet with the thrust of my forearm, wanting to reach beyond our bodies to grab hold of a new space where bodies matter differently.

There's a whip dangling by its strap from a wrist, the knot at its butt end slapping rhythmically against the crack of an ass as a fist disappears, reappears, disappears. I have almost lost sight of him. I hear his labored breathing beneath the black hood, think of the smooth-shaven head it covers. On one of the memory shards: the platinum blonde flattop he wore when we met. On a second: Rutger Hauer in the rooftop scene in *Blade Runner,* in another fantasy of Los Angeles at night. I watch Hauer morph into Daryl Hannah before the two cinematic cyborg bodies merge with his and mine. Media-saturated memory fragments combine. They achieve ambience with our corporealized present and project us into a desired future produced through this very process of subjective transformation.

It is too often impossible to be transsexual in this world, too easy to be worn away by all the petty stigmata of daily living. Elsewhere, on the horizon, another prospect hovers at the vanishing point. Straying into the City of Night, hip-hop sex music carrying us from Sunset Strip to Times Square to the Tenderloin, each of us as tangible and phantasmatic as the urban dreamscape spread before us, we pause only long enough to spray-paint our names on the walls of the sensorium before we disappear into the darkness.

Somewhere, smooth muscle spasms around my fist, and I'm happy. I have no idea what made him come. He reaches for a postcoital cigarette, smoke rising into the night in a parody of movie clichés. I bask in his glow. In the distance, more police helicopters are circling, watching the horizon. It's almost time to go.

Contributors

Roberto Bedoya is a writer, curator, and arts administrator, whose recent poems and essays have appeared in the *Hungry Mind Review, Five Fingers Review, Framework,* and *ZYZZYVA*. Currently, he is the executive director of the National Association of Artists' Organizations, a national arts service organization based in Washington, D.C.

Kaucyila Brooke is an artist who produces photo and text narratives for installation and publication and who also works in video art. She lives in Los Angeles with her Brittany spaniel, Kiki Parker, and teaches in the photography program at CalArts.

Lawrence Chua was born in Penang, Malaysia. He is the recipient of a fellowship from the New York Foundation for the Arts, and his writing has appeared in anthologies including *Charlie Chan Is Dead: Contemporary Asian American Fiction* (Penguin) and *Taking Liberties* (Richard Kaysak), as well as in the *Village Voice, Rolling Stone, The Nation, Vibe, Artforum, Out, BOMB, Muae,* and *Details.* A founding member of Radio Bandung, his radio documentaries and commentaries have aired on National Public Radio and Pacifica Radio.

Linnea Due is the author of three novels (*High and Outside, Give Me Time,* and *Life Savings*) and of *Joining the Tribe: Growing up Gay and Lesbian in the '90s* and is the coeditor of *Dagger: On Butch Women.* She lives in Berkeley, California.

Sandra Lee Golvin is a Los Angeles–based poet and performance and ceremonial artist who tours nationally as a performance artist, creating solo works and collaborative pieces with the award-winning group Queer Rites. Her poems, short stories, and essays have appeared in a number of journals and anthologies, and she has just completed her first novel, *Speaking the Language of the Dead,* a more or less true story about life, love, and linguistics in the City of the Angels at the end of the second millennium.

Jewelle Gomez is the author of a collection of essays, *Forty-Three Septembers,* several books of poetry, including the most recent, *Oral Tradition* and a novel, *The Gilda Stories.* She was on the founding board of GLAAD and currently lives in San Francisco. Her new book of short stories is *Don't Explain* (Firebrand Books).

Francisco J. Gonzalez is a psychiatrist on the clinical faculty at the University of California at San Francisco. He works in a community mental health clinic, Instituto Familiar de la Raza, and also in private practice. He has written on HIV prevention and Latino gay and bisexual men.

Della Grace (aka Del(la) Grace Volcano) is a self-proclaimed Drag King. S/he was educated at the San Francisco Art Institute and the University of Derby. S/he is the author of *Love Bites;* his/her photographs have appeared in numerous books and magazines. His/her first one man show opened in Braganz, Austria, in 1996. Del currently resides in North London.

Amber Hollibaugh is the national field director for Women's Educational Services at GMHC in New York, where she formerly directed the Lesbian AIDS Project. She is a filmmaker, activist, writer, and high femme.

Robert Jensen teaches journalism and media courses at the University of Texas at Austin, where he has been an assistant professor since 1992. His research interests include feminist and lesbian/gay issues in media, law, and ethics. He is coeditor (with David S. Allen) of *Freeing the First Amendment: Critical Perspectives on Freedom of Expression* (New York University Press, 1995) and coauthor (with Gail Dines and Ann Russo) of the forthcoming *Pornography: The Production and Consumption of Inequality* (Routledge, 1998).

Kate Kane is an assistant professor of communications at DePaul University, where she teaches media and cultural studies. She is the author of "The Ideology of Freshness in Feminine Hygiene Commercials," forthcoming in *Feminist Television Criticism* (Oxford University Press, 1997).

Elizabeth A. Kelly is an associate professor of political science at DePaul University, where she teaches courses in political theory and women's studies. She is the author of *Education, Democracy, and Public Knowledge* (Westview Press, 1995), which won the Michael Harrington Award for Best Book of 1995 from the Caucus for a New Political Science of the American Political Science Association.

Monica Majoli is an artist living in Los Angeles. She is represented by the Galerie Air de Paris in Paris and has shown in major museums and galleries in the United States and abroad. Her work has been reviewed in *Artforum, Art Issues, Art in America,* and other publications and is included in *The Absolut Book* (1996) and the catalog for the University Art Museum's exhibition, *In a Different Light* (1996).

Mimi McGurl directs plays, teaches, and studies theater. She lives in San Francisco with her boyfriend Nat.

Sara Miles is a reporter and editor who lives in San Francisco. She is a contributing writer for *OUT* magazine, a freelance contributor to magazines including *The Nation, The New Yorker,* and *Wired,* and editor of the New Thinking series on revolutionary movements in the Third World for the Transnational Institute (Amsterdam).

Robert Reid-Pharr teaches in the English department at Johns Hopkins University.

Eric Rofes is a doctoral student at the University of California at Berkeley's Graduate School of Education, where he teaches the course "Gay and Lesbian Issues in Schools." His most recent book is *Reviving the Tribe: Regenerating Gay Men's Sexuality and Culture in the Ongoing Epidemic* (Haworth, 1996). He lives in San Francisco.

Gayle Rubin got her Ph.D in anthropology from the University of Michigan and is currently teaching in the Women's Studies Department at the University of California at Santa Cruz. Her collected essays will be published by the University of California Press. She is working on a book about gay male leather in San Francisco and a book on the feminist sex wars.

Lawrence Schimel is the author or editor of eighteen books, including *Switch Hitters: Lesbians Write Gay Male Erotica* and *Gay Men Write Lesbian Erotica* (with Carol Queen; Cleis Press 1996), *Food for Life and Other Dish* (Cleis Press, 1996), *Two Hearts Desire: Gay Couples on Their Love* (with Michael Lassell; St. Martin's Press, 1997), and *The Drag Queen of Elfland and Other Stories* (Ultra-Violet Library, 1997). His writings can be found in numerous periodicals and in more than one hundred anthologies.

Richard Schimpf lives in San Francisco with his ex-wife and two dogs.

Susan Stryker received her Ph.D. in history from the University of California at Berkeley in 1992. She is a part-time academic, a freelance writer, and a transgender activist. She is the coauthor of *Gay by the Bay: A History of Queer Culture in the Bay Area* (with Jim Van Buskirk, Chronicle Books, 1996) and the author of a forthcoming book on transgender theory from Oxford University Press.

Index

Index

Index

Index

Index